BANKING
IN THE U.S.:
an annotated bibliography

by
Jean Deuss

The Scarecrow Press, Inc.
Metuchen, N.J., & London
1990

British Library Cataloguing-in-Publication data available

Library of Congress Cataloging-in-Publication Data

Deuss, Jean.
    Banking in the U.S. : an annotated bibliography /
    by Jean Deuss.
        p.   cm.
    Includes indexes.
    ISBN 0-8108-2348-9 (alk. paper)
    1. Banks and banking—United States—Bibliography.
        I. Title.
    Z7164.F5D48   1990
    [HG2461]
    016.3321′0973—dc20   90-9069

CONTENTS

INTRODUCTION

After World War II there was a reexamination of the organization of the government and its agencies, including the banking regulators. Beginning with the Hoover Commission in 1949, the Commission on Money and Credit in 1961, and subsequent studies, almost every aspect of our banking structure has been studied. Not since the banking crisis of 1933 has the fundamental structure of the U.S. banking system been so challenged. The recommendations of these studies has had considerable influence on future legislation. The Bank Holding Company Act of 1956 was the first important banking legislation since the Banking Act of 1935. Bowing to the pressures of increased competition and technological innovation, Congress legislated major changes in bank regulation in the 1960s, 1970s and 1980s. These changes have resulted in an increase in the number of bank holding companies and an easing of money transfers which have lowered state barriers. Nonbank financial institutions are able to offer many banking services formerly provided only by commercial banks. Deregulation of interest rates, while increasing the ability of banks to compete for funds, unfortunately also contributed to the crisis in the savings and loan industry.

The revolution in the banking industry has brought about an increase in the study of our financial institutions. Academic curricula have expanded to include courses in the structure of the financial system and in bank and financial management. Scholars have responded with texts, commentaries and recommendations for change.

Audience

This bibliography is a listing of basic books in the history, organization, regulation and management of U.S. banks and banking for those working on a research project: the scholar, teacher or student; for the practicing banker or others concerned with the financial services industry who need to know the background of a current situation, and the implications for the future; for the librarian who must build a banking collection or augment a business library with information in the banking field.

My experience of over twenty years in the Research Library of the Federal Reserve Bank of New York has given me a knowledge of the literature in the field and the books that interest the scholar and assist the practitioner working in the field. However, I do not presume to be a scholar able to evaluate critically the books included in this list.

Scope and Limitations

The focus of the bibliography is on recent books published in English. Except for a section designed to provide historical background, the books included have been published since 1984.

The emphasis is on the banking industry: commercial banking, savings institutions and investment banking, their operation, regulation and management. Studies on monetary policy and interest rate theory are omitted. Books included on the Federal Reserve System are those that discuss its place in the banking system and its relationship to the banking industry.

There are very few books on banking in individual states. Statistical data can be found in the annual reports of each state's banking department, and in the data published by the government regulatory agencies and by some commercial publishers such as Seshunoff and Decision Research Corporation. The services of Prentice-Hall, Commerce Clearing House and others provide up-to-date regulatory and legislative information for each state.

The bibliography includes only published monographs. Many unpublished working papers, research papers and theses are indexed in online services or listed in institutional journals.

I have not included congressional hearings and reports. The House and Senate banking committees have published listings of those published between 1865 and 1964. Later and current congressional activities are indexed in the Monthly Catalog of Government Publications and the Congressional Information Service Index and Abstracts.

There is a wealth of periodical literature that I have omitted because it is well indexed in both published and online services.

Sources

Sources available to me were the Research Library of the Federal Reserve Bank of New York, the Economics Division of the Research Libraries of the New York Public Library and NYPL's Mid-Manhattan branch, and the library of the American Bankers Association.

Public libraries throughout the United States are augmenting their business collections. Some academic

libraries and a few special libraries make their
collections available to the public. The Board of
Governors of the Federal Reserve System and the
twelve Federal Reserve Banks have libraries. Access to
them varies with each institution, but all have public
information offices that answer inquiries on the
Federal Reserve System. The libraries or information
services of the trade associations such as the American
Bankers Association, Bank Marketing Association
and the American Institute of Bankers are generally
limited to members, but special arrangements may be
made on request. In all cases it is easier to use libraries
if you know what is available for your particular
search. This bibliography attempts to provide that
information.

Arrangement

The bibliography is arranged by broad subjects.
The first three chapters include texts on the U.S.
banking system and international banking, the history
of banking in America and the Federal Reserve
System.

Chapters Four to Six deal with commercial banking,
investment banking and savings institutions.

Chapters Seven, Eight and Nine are concerned with
banking laws and regulations, bank management and
bank automation.

Chapter Ten is a short listing of books of statistical
compilations. Other statistical information is found in
yearbooks, periodical releases of governmental agencies, and from online services.

Chapters Eleven to Twelve list reference sources,
periodicals and newspapers and services both printed
and online. Periodical listings show, by abbreviation,
where they are indexed and if available online.

The Appendixes include acronyms and abbreviations, a chronology of major banking legislation and studies, and a listing of regulatory agencies and trade associations.

I have tried to make the entries perfect in every bibliographic respect, and any errors and omissions are my responsibility alone.

I am grateful to staff members and former staff members of the Federal Reserve Bank of New York: George Budzeika and Joseph Scherer, who reviewed my initial listing and gave help with the scope and focus of the work; Emily Trueblood, Chief Librarian of the Research Library, Roberta G. Laskowitz, Chief Law Librarian, and their staffs, who gave me special access to those collections. I give special thanks to William Hegeman, who prepared the indexes. The New York Public Library has immense resources and I found Mary Margaret Regan and Milada Klatil especially helpful. Joan E. Gervino and the staff of the library of the American Bankers Association helped to fill in gaps not readily available in New York. Mary McNierney Grant and Doris Schild provided much critical and proofreading assistance. Finally, I thank Jeanne Morrow for her encouragement and support. To all I am most grateful.

JEAN DEUSS
Chief Librarian, Retired
Research Library
Federal Reserve Bank of New York

1. GENERAL TEXTS

1. Auerbach, Robert D. *Money, Banking, and Financial Markets.* 3d ed. New York: Macmillan, 1988. 832p.
   Emphasizes the theory and application of the operation of the financial markets. Describes the financial intermediaries, especially the depository institutions, and the Federal Reserve System. Presents a thorough analysis of the arithmetic of asset price income and interest rates. There are notes and a glossary at the end of each chapter.

2. Bowden, Elbert V. *Money, Banking, and the Financial System.* St. Paul, MN: West, 1989. 765p.
   Entry-level text includes events through 1987. As the subtitle states, it is a "conceptual explanation of the nature and functions of money, of financial institutions, instruments and markets, and of macro-monetary theory and policy."

3. Campbell, Colin D.; Campbell, Rosemary G.; and Dolan, Edwin G. *Money, Banking, and Monetary Policy.* Chicago: Dryden, 1988. 617p.
   Up-to-date text that examines the current status of money and banking, describes the new financial innovations, and reviews the recent changes in government regulation. Illustrated by "real world" data. Presents a historical perspective which is amplified by quotations of people who have shaped our monetary history. Also gives wide coverage of banking with a focus on banking

stability. Discusses current debates on economic and monetary theory. Includes selected references at the end of each chapter and a glossary.

4. Friedman, David H. *Money & Banking*. 2d ed. Washington, DC: American Bankers Association, 1989. 500p.

   Designed as a text for the introductory course at the American Institute of Bankers, can also be used by experienced bankers to prepare for advanced courses. Explains the function of money and the role of banking in the economy, the part banking plays in carrying out monetary policy, the operation and regulation of banks, international banking; and projects the future banking trends.

5. Goldfeld, Stephen M., and Chandler, Lester V. *The Economics of Money and Banking*. 8th ed. New York: Harper, 1981. 628p.

   For many years this has been a standard text for those students beginning their formal study of money and banking. Earlier editions were written by Professor Chandler, and in this edition Professor Goldfeld, as principal author, continues the original focus of the book on the most important principles, processes and problems of money and banking, treated from an institutional and historical point of view. Selected readings follow most chapters.

6. Horvitz, Paul M., and Ward, Richard A. *Monetary Policy and the Financial System*. 6th ed. Englewood Cliffs, NJ: Prentice-Hall, 1987. 532p.

   A basic text for students of financial institutions and money and banking with considerable attention to monetary policy. Deals with the structure, operation and regulation of the financial system.

There are selected readings at the end of each chapter and a glossary.

7. Kamerschen, David R. *Money & Banking.* 9th ed. Cincinnati, OH: South-Western Publishing Co., 1988. 663p.

    A beginning text that examines the transitional status of financial institutions in general and banking in particular in a historical perspective. Major portions of the book are devoted to contemporary economic theory, monetary and fiscal policies, regulation, and institutions. There is a full discussion of the Monetary Control Act of 1980 and the Garn-St Germain Act.

8. Kaufman, George G. *The U.S. Financial System: Money, Markets, and Institutions.* 4th ed. Englewood Cliffs, NJ: Prentice-Hall, 1989. 732p.

    This introductory text presents a thorough overview of the operations of the financial system. Describes commercial bank and nonbank financial institutions. Discusses current topics in financial markets and institutions. Deals with international banking and monetary theory and policy. References to additional readings are at the end of each chapter.

9. Khambata, Dara M. *The Practice of Multinational Banking; Macro-Policy Issues and Key International Concepts.* New York: Quorum, 1986. 269p.

    Designed for practitioners and students who want to become more familiar with the theory and practice of international banking. Describes the development of multinational banks focusing on the policy and concept-oriented issues in the area of international banking. Explains the regulation, market factors and operation of multinational banks. There are bibliographic references at the end of each chapter.

10. Lewis, M. K., and Davis, K. T. *Domestic and International Banking.* Cambridge, MA: MIT Press, 1987. 440p.

Describes the operation of modern banking, and points out the essential similarities between activities of most financial institutions. In addition to the chapters on traditional activities of banking, book deals with recent developments, such as the spread of banking beyond domestic markets, the related growth of wholesale banking, and the movement into the range of off-balance sheet business. Illustrated by comparisons of banking in the United Kingdom, United States and Australia. Bibliography contains books and articles, there is a glossary.

11. Meyer, Paul A. *Money, Financial Institutions and the Economy.* Homewood, IL: Irwin, 1986. 755p.

Designed for Junior/Senior level business students, the text blends economic theory with institutional and historical material. One of the highlights of the book is the discussion of the relationship between regulatory policies and financial structure. Good general text for those who are not experts, but need to know about the current issues in banking.

12. Miller, Roger LeRoy, and Pulsinelli, Robert W. *Modern Money & Banking.* 2d ed. New York: McGraw-Hill, 1989. 633p.

Up-to-date text that incorporates the large number of bank failures and the insolvency of the FSLIC. Describes the new credit instruments and the growth of the large-dollar payments system. Deals with the instability of the financial markets and the stock market crash of 1987. Includes recent legislation.

13. Oppenheim, Peter K. *International Banking*. 5th ed. Washington, DC: American Bankers Association, 1987. 398p.

    Designed as an introductory text or for those who need up-to-date information on U.S. commercial banks' international operations. This edition reflects the situation of the 80s, including new products and new techniques to meet changing demands. Describes a bank's role in foreign trade, foreign exchange and funds transfer or payments. Illustrated by actual forms used in foreign transactions. There is a reading list, also references at the end of each chapter.

14. Prochnow, Herbert V. *American Financial Institutions*. New York: Prentice-Hall, 1951. 799p.

    Collection of essays by leaders in the financial world. Designed to give students an understanding of all major American financial institutions, their function, relationships, methods of operation and distinct services. Even though it is old, this remains a basic text and offers a good background for the study of banking and related institutions. There are suggested readings at the end of each essay.

15. Ritter, Lawrence S., and Silber, William L. *Principles of Money, Banking and Financial Markets*. 6th ed. New York: Basic Books, 1989. 660p.

    Introductory text presents the basics of the business of financial intermediaries and the art of central banking. Includes chapters on financial

instruments, financial innovation, international
debt problems, and floating rate loans. Epilogue
discusses careers in banking and the financial
markets. Includes glossary and suggested readings.

16. Spellman, Lewis J. *The Depository Firm and Indus-
    try: Theory, History, and Regulation.* New York:
    Academic Press, 1982. 397p.

    The author states, "This volume has a point of
    view. Commercial banks, savings and loan associ-
    ations, mutual savings banks, and credit unions
    are dealt with much like firms in any other
    industry. They purchase resources, produce a
    product and price that product. The firms
    operate in an environment constrained by com-
    petition and regulation." Spellman develops this
    thesis using a historical and analytical approach.
    He discusses the political environment, competi-
    tion, the market and the regulatory forces that
    shaped the depository industry.
    He uses microeconomic models to describe de-
    pository firms and industry, and analyzes the
    effect of the financial system on the economy.
    There is a bibliography at the end of each
    chapter.

2. HISTORY

17. Advisory Committee on Banking. *National Banks and the Future. Report . . . to the Comptroller of the Currency.* Washington, DC: Government Printing Office, 1962. 189p.

    Known as the Saxon Report, one of the first post World War II studies looking for reform of the banking system. Surveyed national banks for opinions concerning needed changes in laws, policies and regulations affecting their operations. Makes recommendations covering almost every aspect of commercial banking.

18. Burns, Helen M. *The American Banking Community and the New Deal Banking Reforms, 1933–1935.* Westport, CT: Greenwood, 1974. 203p.

    Ms. Burns, formerly Chief of the Federal Reserve Bank of New York Law Library, wrote this book as her MBA thesis for New York University. She focuses on those New Deal laws that apply directly to bank reform, and shows how the banking community and the Roosevelt Administration's policies interacted to bring about the reform legislation.

19. Carosso, Vincent P. *Investment Banking in America: A History.* Harvard Studies in Business History, V. 25. Cambridge, MA: Harvard University Press, 1970. 569p.

    A historical treatment of the origins and development of the investment banking business from 1873 to the 1960s. Identifies the forces that prompted change from primarily financing the burgeoning railroad business in the late 1800s to underwriting new industries by 1900. Shows the ways investment firms adapted their operations to alterations in the economic, social and political environment. Describes the industry during the period between World War I and World War II, and the effect of regulations governing it. There is an extensive bibliography, including private papers, published and unpublished, and documents, books and articles.

20. Clarke, M. St. Clair, and Hall, D. A., comps. *Legislative and Documentary History of the Bank of the United States; Including the Original Bank of North America.* Reprint of original published in Washington, DC: Gales & Section, 1832. New York: Augustus Kelly, 1967. 832p.

   Important collection of source material on the Bank of North America which was chartered by the Continental Congress, and the First and Second United States Bank which were early attempts at central banking in the United States.

21. Commission on Money and Credit. *Money and Credit: Their Influence on Jobs, Prices, and Growth; Report.* Englewood Cliffs, NJ: Prentice-Hall, 1961. 285p.

   The Commission was established by the Committee for Economic Development to study the U.S. monetary and financial system. Study was supported by a number of monographs by scholars and institutions. Among those were: American Bankers Association, *The Commercial Banking Industry,* and Leon T. Kendall, *The*

Savings and Loan Business. Report discusses strengths and limitations of various kinds of policy measures, makes recommendations including the organizational structure needed to bring about policy changes.

22. Dewey, Davis Rich. *Financial History of the United States.* llth ed. New York: Longmans, Green, 1931. 581p.

    Still a standard text of the history of U.S. public finance from the colonial period to 1930. Uses a broad definition of financial history to include some considerations of the monetary system such as coinage and bank issues. Also includes a historical section on investment banking. Introductory section is a lengthy bibliography.

23. Fenstermaker, Joseph Van. *The Development of American Commercial Banking, 1782–1837.* Kent, OH: Kent State University Bureau of Economic and Business Research, 1965. 247p.

    The author's PhD thesis, submitted to the University of Illinois in 1963, is concerned with the financial history and economic analysis of the U.S. prior to 1860. Supported by considerable statistical data not found in other histories of this early period. There is a thorough review of the literature of both secondary and primary sources.

24. Fischer, Gerald C. *American Banking Structure.* New York: Columbia University Press, 1968. 429p.

    A study financed by the Ford Foundation and the American Bankers Association to provide background material for investigations of the banking structure. Focuses on the history of unit, branch, chain, correspondent and group banking. When this study was commissioned, the ABA thought that the evolution of banking technology, shortage of qualified management personnel and enlarged financial requirements of the economy and changes in banking regulation would force the Government and the banking industry to make a choice regarding the form of banking structure that would prevail nationally. The bibliography includes articles and monographs.

25. Hammond, Bray. *Banks and Politics in America from the Revolution to the Civil War.* Princeton, NJ: Princeton University Press, 1957. 771p.

Traces the influence that two rival forces in the early nineteenth century had upon the development of American banking. The author's thesis is that the political and cultural forces of business enterprise and the opposing force of agrarianism fought to influence the type of banking system because banks provide credit. Since business made the most prosperous use of borrowed funds, the shape of the banking industry, as it developed, reflected the needs of business. There is an extensive bibliography.

26. Kennedy, Susan Estabrook. *The Banking Crisis of 1933.* Lexington, KY: University Press of Kentucky, 1973. 270p.

A narrative account of the events of 1930 to 1933 that led to the passage of the Banking Act of 1933. The bibliography contains references to manuscript collections, oral history memoirs, government documents, as well as books and articles.

27. Klebaner, Benjamin J. *Commercial Banking in the U.S.: A History.* Hinsdale, IL: Dryden, 1974. 202p.

A concise treatment of the evolution of American commercial banking practice, structure and regulation from the beginning of the late eighteenth century to the present day. Includes bibliography.

28. Knox, John Jay. *A History of Banking in the United States.* New York: Bradford Rhodes, 1903. 880p.

    Mr. Knox was Comptroller of the Currency for many years. Basing much of the material and the statistics on his annual reports, he completed most of Part I on national banks before his death. Other authors wrote the sections in Part II dealing with state banks. A thorough analysis of the laws that governed the national and state banks in the nineteenth century.

29. Krooss, Herman E., ed. *Documentary History of Banking and Currency in the United States.* New York: Chelsea House, 1969. 4 vols.

    First comprehensive documentary history since study done in 1910 by Huntington and Mawhinney for the National Monetary Commission, and the earlier study by Clarke and Hall in 1832. Contains over 300 documents. Text is divided into ten historical periods beginning with 1637 when wampum was established as legal tender.

30. Krooss, Herman E., and Blyn, Martin R. *A History of Financial Intermediaries.* New York: Random House, 1971. 254p.

    A historical summary of all financial institutions, not just banks, from the earliest period in American history to 1970. Concern is with the borrowers and lenders and the process by which the two were brought together. Contains notes on sources. Earlier study by Studenski and Krooss,

Financial History of the United States, can serve as a companion volume.

31. Manning, James Hilton. *A Century of American Savings Banks; Published under the Auspices of the Savings Banks Association of the State of New York, in Commemoration of the Centenary of Savings Banks in America.* New York: B. F. Buck, 1917. 2 vols.

    Traces the rise of savings banks in Europe and the development of the thrift movement in America. Presents a history of each of the so-called pioneer savings banks in the United States including school and Postal Savings Banks. The second volume is a history of each of the 141 savings banks in the State of New York at the time.

32. Nadler, Marcus, and Bogen, Jules I. *The Banking Crisis: The End of an Epoch.* New York: Dodd, Mead, 1933. 202p.

    A contemporary account of the events that led to the banking crisis of 1933. Professors Nadler and Bogen present a clear and concise explanation of why the crisis occurred.

33. President's Commission on Financial Structure and Regulation. *Report; Including Recommendations of the Department of the Treasury.* Washington, DC: U.S. Senate. Committee on Banking, Housing and Urban Affairs, 1973. 213p.

    Known as the Hunt Commission, the report focuses on regulatory problems of commercial banks, savings and loan associations, mutual savings banks, credit unions, life insurance companies, and pension funds. Its recommendations, incorporated to some extent in the Treasury Department's recommendations for legislation, cover a wide range of activities affecting financial institutions. Many of the Hunt Commission's recommendations were also included in the FINE study and influenced the legislation that led to the Depository Institutions Deregulation and Monetary Control Act of 1980.

34. Redlich, Fritz. *The Molding of American Banking; Men and Ideas.* New York: Johnson Reprint Corp., 1968. 517p.

   Part I, originally published in 1947, deals with the period from 1781 to 1840 and describes the bank founders and personnel. There are chapters on early American central banking, free banking, southern plantation banks and savings banks. Part II, originally published in 1951, concerns the process by which American banking became what it was prior to the establishment of the Federal Reserve. Discusses the problems of clearing and the origins of the Clearing House. Describes the rise of private banks and the development of investment banking. The appendix is a biography of George S. Coe, leading nineteenth century banker and innovator. There is a bibliography at the end of each part; and the introduction to the reprint edition reviews the literature published since the original publication.

35. Studenski, Paul, and Krooss, Herman E. *Financial History of the United States: Fiscal, Monetary, Banking, and Tariff; Including Financial Administration and State and Local Finance.* 2d ed. New York: McGraw-Hill, 1963. 605p.

   Traces the development of American finance emphasizing the interrelationships and effects of government fiscal, monetary and banking policies and institutional arrangements from the colonial period to the 1960s. There is an extensive bibliography. See also Krooss and Blyn, *A History of Financial Intermediaries,* which has a fuller treatment of the post World War II period.

36. Sumner, William Graham. *A History of Banking in the United States.* A History of Banking in All the Leading Nations, v. 1. New York: Journal of Commerce and Commercial Bulletin, 1896. 485p.

    One of the classics of American banking history. Details the colonial experiment with joint stock banks and the continuation of the colonial ideal of state banks being institutions based either on the "faith and credit" of the state alone or a combination of public funds and private subscription. Traces the rise of local banks and the attempts by the federal government to regulate banking and currency. The book does not go beyond the establishment of a national banking system in 1863.

37. U.S. Congress. House. Committee on Banking, Currency and Housing. *FINE: Financial Institutions and the Nation's Economy. Compendium of Papers Prepared for the FINE Study.* Washington, DC: Government Printing Office, 1976. 2 vols.

    Papers prepared according to the discussion principles laid down by the Committee. They deal with the depository institutions and the housing situation and their regulation, the structure and operation of the Federal Reserve System, and international banking. Contain proposals for the restructuring of our financial institutions. Along with the Hunt Report, the FINE Report influenced subsequent legislation.

38. U.S. Monetary Commission, 1876. *Report and Accompanying Documents.* Washington, DC: Government Printing Office, 1877–1879. 2 vols.

The Commission was charged with inquiring into the current situation of the country. Instrumental in finally disposing of the question of free silver. Work done by the people on this commission started the studies that led to the recommendation for the establishment of the Federal Reserve System.

39. U.S. National Monetary Commission. *Publications.* Washington, DC: Government Printing Office, 1910–1912. 24 vols.

Exhaustive survey of the banking systems of Europe and the United States. Volume 2 concerns the financial laws of the United States from 1778–1909. Volume 4 describes banking in the United States before the Civil War. Volume 5 examines the national banking system. Volume 6 discusses clearing house and instruments. Volume 7 describes state bank trust companies and the independent Treasury system. Volume 24 transmits the report to Congress and includes the Aldrich Plan which led to the legislation establishing the Federal Reserve System.

40. White, Horace. *Money and Banking, Illustrated by American History; Revised and Continued to the Year 1914.* 5th ed. New York: Ginn, 1914. 541p.

Important early text places the operation of the American banking system in a historical context, beginning with banking in colonial times through to the establishment of the Federal Reserve System.

3. FEDERAL RESERVE SYSTEM

41. Beckhart, Benjamin Haggott. *Federal Reserve System*. New York: American Institute of Banking, 1972. 584p.

    Basic text describes the Federal Reserve System. Although there have been some significant changes in the banking system and the functions of the regulatory agencies since this book was written, it is still where one should begin in order to gain an understanding of the Federal Reserve System. Beckhart's approach is historical, beginning with the origins of the Federal Reserve and its administrative structure; continuing with discussions of certain crucial periods during the years 1913 to 1960 and the 1960s; going on with the Fed's international monetary activities; and closing with an analysis of monetary instruments and the goals of monetary policy. Bibliographic notes at the end of each chapter. There is an extensive glossary and index.

42. Brown, Weir M. *Keeping the Central Bank Central: U.S. Monetary Policy and the Banking System*. Boulder, CO: Westview, 1987. 103p.

    In recent years there have been profound changes in the nature and composition of deposits at depository institutions, as well as legislation regarding reserve requirements. The author discusses how these changes have affected the relationship between the banking system and the

Federal Reserve in regard to the conduct of national monetary policy. He makes concluding observations and recommendations. There are notes at the end of each chapter and a bibliography.

43. Clark, Lawrence E. *Central Banking under the Federal Reserve System; with Special Consideration of the Federal Reserve Bank of New York.* New York: Macmillan, 1935. 437p.

    An account of the development of the Federal Reserve System during its first twenty years of existence. Focuses on the evolution of its central bank functions as carried out by the Federal Reserve Bank of New York. There is a useful bibliography for the early history of the Federal Reserve System.

44. Clifford, A. Jerome. *The Independence of the Federal Reserve System.* Philadelphia, PA: University of Pennsylvania Press, 1965. 435p.

    The Fed's independence has been an issue since the beginning of its founding. The division of authority between the Treasury and the Federal Reserve Board was not resolved until the accord in 1951. Congress from time to time has sought to limit the power of the Board. This book details issues and the problems. Bibliography lists government documents, Federal Reserve publications and papers, and books.

45. DeRosa, Paul, and Stern, Gary H. *In the Name of Money: A Professional's Guide to the Federal Reserve, Interest Rates, and Money.* New York: McGraw-Hill, 1981. 172p.

    DeRosa and Stern, two veterans of the Fed, here present a concise guide for the professional

about the Federal Reserve System. They empha-
size the market function of the Fed, how monetary policy affects jobs and the economy and how
its international operations affect domestic policy. The last chapter summarizes the book and is
designed to be used as a handbook. There is a
glossary.

46. de Saint Phalle, Thibaut. *The Federal Reserve; an
   International Mystery.* New York: Praeger, 1985.
   314p.
      Purpose is to help people understand the Fed,
   especially its conduct of monetary policy and its
   regulatory activities at home and abroad. Seeks to
   determine whether the Federal Reserve Board
   has carried out its purpose with respect to
   monetary policy and what changes should be
   made in the regulatory structure. Bibliography
   includes books, articles and public documents.

47. *The Federal Reserve System: Purposes & Functions.*
   7th ed. Washington, DC: Board of Governors of
   the Federal Reserve System, 1984. 120p.
      A general picture of the structure of the
   Federal Reserve System written for the nonpro-
   fessional. Useful for quick reference.

48. Garcia, Gillian G., and Plantz, Elizabeth. *The
   Federal Reserve, Lender of Last Resort.* Cambridge,
   MA: Ballinger, 1988. 310p.
      Explores the concept and development of the
   federal government as the lender of last resort as
   carried out by the Federal Reserve System.
   Questions whether changing conditions in the
   world financial system require a revision of
   procedures for providing immediate liquidity in a
   financial crisis. Establishes criteria for evaluating

the Fed's performance as lender of last resort in the 1970s. Illustrated by several case studies such as the Franklin National Bank. Discusses the present issues and future execution of lender of last resort activities.

49. Greider, William. *Secrets of the Temple: How the Federal Reserve Runs the Country.* New York: Simon and Schuster, 1987. 798p.

This book has aroused considerable controversy. The author maintains that the Federal Reserve's independent status gives it tremendous economic and political power over which the general public has no control. This power, he maintains, can lead to monetary decisions that are not always in the best interest of the people as a whole. Greider has written this book with the intent of demystifying the Fed so as to allow for more public influence on its activities. Each chapter is annotated.

50. Hadjimichalakis, Michael G. *The Federal Reserve, Money and Interest Rates; The Volcker Years and Beyond.* New York: Praeger, 1985. 273p.

A fairly technical discussion of the Federal Reserve System's structure, goals, decision making, operating and reporting procedures. Describes the financial and economic setting at the time of Paul Volcker's appointment as chairman; and analyzes how the innovations such as NOW accounts and other changes in the financial market have affected the Fed's policy making in recent years. There is an extensive bibliography and a glossary of monetary and financial terms.

51. Kettl, Donald F. *Leadership at the Fed.* New Haven, CT: Yale University Press, 1986. 218p.

The Federal Reserve System, particularly its

Board of Governors, in all the years of its existence has come under fire for its power and independence. This book analyzes the way each chairman, some more than others, have had to deal with the President, the Congress, the Treasury and various other critics and adversaries on these two issues. Shows how the philosophies of the Fed's leaders have shaped the institution over the years.

52. Laughlin, J. Laurence. *The Federal Reserve Act; Its Origin and Problems*. New York: Macmillan, 1933. 400p.

Laughlin, an opponent of Free Silver, worked to defeat Bryan. He organized the National Citizens League to educate the American public on currency and banking issues. This is a personal account of the story of the Aldrich Plan and the Glass Bill and the political stages that led to the establishment of the Federal Reserve System.

53. Livingston, James. *Origin of the Federal Reserve System: Money, Class, and Corporate Capitalism, 1890–1913*. Ithaca, NY: Cornell University Press, 1986. 250p.

A look at the banking and monetary reform movement at the turn of the century as a social phenomenon rather than as a response to economic factors that required structural changes in the banking system. Livingston's theory differs from those of Timberlake, West and White. The four books should be read together for modern scholarly views of the bank reform movement and the establishment of the Federal Reserve System.

54. Melton, William C. *Inside the Fed: Making Monetary Policy*. Homewood, IL: Dow Jones-Irwin, 1985. 226p.

Aimed at those with only a minimal economics background, tells the story of monetary policy in recent years—what went right and what went wrong. Seeks to demystify the policy functions of the Federal Reserve. There are notes at the end of each chapter and a glossary.

55. Prochnow, Herbert V., ed. *The Federal Reserve System.* New York: Harper, 1960. 393p.

Standard book of readings. Contains papers contributed by leading bankers and economists. As with Beckhart, the essays, though written before 1960, are basic to an understanding of the Federal Reserve System. Includes bibliography.

56. Timberlake, Richard H., Jr. *The Origins of Central Banking in the United States.* Cambridge, MA: Harvard University Press, 1978. 272p.

Principal conclusion of the book is that central banking was made, not born, and that it evolved as a pragmatic and opportunistic action when favorable circumstances set the stage. Author questions necessity of central banks as institutions.

57. Warburg, Paul M. *The Federal Reserve System: Its Origins and Growth; Reflections and Recollections.* New York: Macmillan, 1930. 2 vols.

Mr. Warburg, a leading Wall Street banker and financier, as a member of the first Federal Reserve Board, was most influential in the early years of the Federal Reserve System. His work is essential source material for scholars of banking and the Federal Reserve. Volume one deals with the origins of the Federal Reserve and its history to 1927. Chapters 21 to 37 contain texts of

important documents. Volume two is a collection
of essays written by Mr. Warburg between 1906
and 1930.

58. West, Robert Craig. *Banking Reform and the Federal
    Reserve, 1863–1923*. Ithaca, NY: Cornell Univer-
    sity Press, 1977. 243p.

    Discussion of the American financial and
    monetary history and the reform attempts which
    culminated in the passage of the Federal Reserve
    Act. West feels that the reform debates came
    down to the question of legitimizing the "real bills
    doctrine" and the choice between a centralized or
    decentralized banking system. Includes a com-
    prehensive bibliography.

59. White, Eugene Nelson. *The Regulation and Reform
    of the American Banking System, 1900–1929*. Prince-
    ton, NJ: Princeton University Press, 1983. 251p.

    A thorough analysis of the dual banking system
    and the reform movement that led to establish-
    ment of the Federal Reserve. White feels that
    independent banks had no incentive to join the
    Federal Reserve System, and the lack of branch
    banking also contributed to weakening the bank-
    ing system. He asserts that deregulation is the key
    to strengthening the banking system rather than
    new agencies or regulations. Includes a bibliogra-
    phy.

60. Willis, Henry Parker. *The Federal Reserve System:
    Legislation, Organization, and Operation*. New York:
    Ronald, 1923. 1765p.

    Professor Willis was Secretary of the Federal
    Reserve Board from 1914 to 1918. He worked
    with the Senate Banking and Currency Commit-
    tee on drafting and passage of the original

Federal Reserve Act and again on preparing the Banking Act of 1933. This book is the first of a three-volume study on the Federal Reserve. A detailed historical account of the adoption of the Federal Reserve Act, of the organization of the Federal Reserve Banks and of the management and direction of the Federal Reserve System under the supervision of the Board.

61. Willis, Henry Parker, and Steiner, William H. *Federal Reserve Banking Practice.* New York: Appleton, 1926. 1016p.

Designed as a handbook of practices for the banker, it is of interest only as part of the whole study in showing how the Federal Reserve operated in the early period.

62. Willis, Henry Parker. *The Theory and Practice of Central Banking; with Special Reference to American Experience, 1923–1935.* New York: Harper & Bros., 1936. 480p.

Traces the evolution of the Federal Reserve as a central banking system.

4. COMMERCIAL BANKING

63. Altman, Edward I., ed., and McKinney, Mary Jane, assoc. ed. *Handbook of Financial Markets and Institutions.* 6th ed. New York: Wiley, 1987. v.p.

    Articles by experts in the field covering the whole range of financial markets. Sections deal with the institutional control of the money and capital markets and Federal Reserve control, the major changes since 1970 in commercial banking, investment banking, savings institutions and international banking. There is a bibliography at the end of each section, and an appendix giving sources of financial and investment information.

64. Baer, Herbert, and Gregorash, Sue F., eds. *Toward Nationwide Banking: A Guide to the Issues.* Chicago: Federal Reserve Bank of Chicago, 1986. 105p.

    Collection of articles on the effects of interstate banking and on the liberalized laws governing intrastate branching. Topics cover various types of interstate banking legislation, legal and economic framework of interstate consolidation, effects of nationwide branching on the banking systems in foreign countries, effects of intrastate branching, the forces driving interstate consolidation, and the likely players in interstate merger activity. Includes references.

65. Baker, Kemper W., Jr. *The Role and Performance of Regional Banks in International Markets.* New Brunswick, NJ, 1983. 153p. Unpublished thesis.

     Thesis for the Stonier Graduate School of Banking, American Bankers Association, at Rutgers University. Analyzes the trends in international banking, especially the entrance of the regional banks into the international markets. Compares the performance of the regional banks with that of the large money market banks in this field. Bibliography includes references to books, articles, papers, reports, speeches and published documents.

66. Bank for International Settlements. *Recent Innovations in International Banking.* Basle, Switzerland, 1986. 270p.

     A report prepared by a study group of the central banks of the Group of Ten countries. The group interviewed international commercial and investment bankers to learn their use of new financial instruments, to discern the broad trends in international financial innovation and the factors influencing such innovation. Report concludes with a study of the issues raised and the impact of financial innovation on financial stability, financial statement and statistical reporting, and on the conduct and effectiveness of monetary policy.

67. Bergsten, C. Fred; Cline, William R.; and Williamson, John. *Bank Lending to Developing Countries: The Policy Alternatives.* Policy Analyses in International Economics, 10. Washington, DC: Institute of International Economics, 1985. 210p.

     Studies the possible changes in the nature and

terms of commercial bank lending to debtor
countries. Twenty-four policy proposals were
considered as to the impact on debtor countries,
on the banks, and on the international financial
system as a whole. Four specific options are
analyzed pro and con. For follow-up on this study
see Cline's *Mobilizing Bank Lending to Debtor
Countries.*

68. Board of Governors of the Federal Reserve
    System. *The Bank Holding Company Movement to
    1978: A Compendium.* Washington, DC, 1978.
    289p.
       A study by the staff of the Federal Reserve
    Board whose purpose is to review and summarize
    available published research on those aspects of
    bank holding company activity that are relevant
    to public policy. The relatively complete and
    documented summary serves as a background for
    discussions on bank holding company regulatory
    and supervisory policy, and as a basis for further
    research. Includes a list of references, mostly to
    journal articles.

69. Board of Governors of the Federal Reserve
    System. *Staff Studies.* Washington, DC, 1965—.
       A series of analytical papers, prepared by
    System staff, relating to banking practices, mone-
    tary and fiscal policy. Titles are listed in the
    Federal Reserve Bulletin.

70. Bowden, Elbert V., and Holbert, Judith L.
    *Revolution in Banking: New Fed Policies, New
    Technology, Legislative/de Facto Deregulation, and
    Powerful Market Forces Bring the Rapid Homogeniza-
    tion of the U.S. Financial Services Industry.* 2d ed.
    Reston, VA: Reston Publishing, 1984. 288p.

As the subtitle indicates this book gives the nonspecialist an overview of the many kinds of changes that have occurred in the financial services industry. It explains the background and events leading to the legislative developments of the 80s, the effect on the industry and the implications for the future. Includes bibliographies and index.

71. Bryan, Lowell L. *Breaking Up the Bank: Rethinking an Industry under Siege*. Homewood, IL: Dow Jones-Irwin, 1988. 209p.

Explains why traditional banking organization is no longer efficient. Suggests a new structure for managing and regulating banks which would divide the depository and lending functions. Banks would build separate businesses around each function which would offer customers the most value for the lowest price, and protect depositors through regulation without subsidizing unsound lending practices. Includes bibliography.

72. Burns, Arthur F. *The Ongoing Revolution in American Banking*. Washington, DC: American Enterprise Institute for Public Policy Research, 1988. 94p.

Paper originally presented on March 17, 1987 at the University of Pittsburgh Bicentennial Colloquium on Changes in International Operation of Economic Factor Markets. Reviews the changes in commercial banking since the 1950s and the state of banking in the 1980s. Discusses the problems facing bank regulators and the vicissitudes of monetary policy. Dr. Burns was a former Federal Reserve Board chairman. This is his last published work.

73. Cargill, Thomas F., and Garcia, Gillian G. *Financial Reform in the 1980's*. Stanford, CA: Hoover Institution Press, 1985. 214p.

    Briefly reviews the financial reforms in our history. Discusses the unstable financial and monetary environment of the 1970s that led to the regulatory and legislative changes of the early 1980s. Describes the major features of these changes. Analyzes additional reforms that will be required to achieve a stable financial and monetary environment for the 1980s. References are mainly to articles and Federal Reserve staff studies.

74. Carson, Deane, ed. *Banking and Monetary Studies*. Homewood, IL: Irwin, 1963. 441p.

    Essays written by leading academicians commemorate the establishment of a system of national banks by Congress in 1863. Includes chapters on banking history, Federal Reserve System and the operation of commercial banks in pre-deregulation times.

75. Channon, Derek F. *Global Banking Strategy*. New York: Wiley, 1988. 389p.

    A broad overview of multinational banking. Describes the evolution of multinational banking, the international capital markets, the effect of industrial development on the banking system, the debt problem, the changing nature of corporate banking, and the impact of regulation and deregulation.

76. Clarke, Stephen V. O. *American Banks in the International Interbank Market*. Salomon Brothers Center for the Study of Financial Institutions

Monograph in Finance and Economics, No. 1983–4. New York: New York University Graduate School of Business Administration, 1984. 58p.

Discusses the increased risks that big banks run in their dealings in the international markets. Too much dependence on government support has led to carelessness in assessing risks and contributed to market instability. Paper outlines the steps that should be taken to minimize the risks and assure financial stability. Includes a bibliography.

77. Cline, William R. *Mobilizing Bank Lending to Debtor Countries.* Policy Analyses in International Economics, 18. Washington, DC: Institute of International Economics, 1987. 92p.

A follow-up on the Benston study, takes a fresh look at possible new approaches to bank lending to debtor countries that could encourage prudent expansion of credit, and discusses additional options and proposals for relief of the debt crisis.

78. Coler, Mark, and Ratner, Ellis M., eds. *Financial Services: Insiders' Views of the Future.* New York: New York Institute of Finance, 1988. 249p.

A series of articles, written by experts, examines the state of the financial services industry today. Deals with new products offered by banks, the entry of banks into the securities market, portfolio management and financial planning, and the marketing and promoting of new services.

79. Compton, Eric N. *Inside Commercial Banking.* 2d ed. New York: Wiley, 1983. 273p.

Objective is to give the general reader and the practitioner in banking contemporary informa-

tion on changes affecting the banking industry.
Discusses the competitive, regulatory, technological and market-related developments that have
changed the nature of the commercial banking
business. Predates the Garn-St Germain Act of
1982. Includes a comprehensive bibliography
and index.

80. Compton, Eric N. *The New World of Commercial
    Banking.* Lexington, MA: Lexington Books,
    1987. 316p.
    Updates the author's earlier book. Emphasizes
    the implications for management of the funda-
    mental changes that have occurred since 1961.
    Among the major changes was the growth of
    interest bearing accounts, such as money market
    deposit accounts. There are extensive references
    to newspaper and magazine articles and a bibliog-
    raphy.

81. Coulbeck, Neil. *The Multinational Banking Indus-
    try.* New York: New York University Press, 1984.
    397p.
    A description of universal multinational banks
    showing their strategic planning, business devel-
    opment and financial constraints. Points out that
    market pressures cause leading banks in all
    developed countries to adopt similar strategies,
    and to compete among themselves. Introductory
    chapters give the background of multinational
    banking and general information on banking
    markets worldwide, followed by chapters on
    those countries that best illustrate universal
    multinational banking.

82. Donaldson, T. H. *Lending in International Commer-
    cial Banking.* 2d ed. London: Macmillan, 1988.
    211p.

Detailed explanation of how banks analyze international credits and how such lending differs from the domestic activity of these banks. Discusses the problems in the documentation and syndication of international loans, and the risks and profitability of such loans. Includes bibliography.

83. Federal Deposit Insurance Corporation. *Mandate for Change: Restructuring of the Banking Industry.* Washington, DC, 1987. 124p.

Examines the issues that are relevant to determining the future role of banking and what role governmental regulatory and supervisory agencies should play in this process. Includes a historical overview of bank powers, concerns relating to new powers and an FDIC proposal to restructure the banking system.

84. Federal Reserve Bank of Atlanta. *Interstate Banking: Strategies for a New Era.* Westport, CT: Quorum, 1985. 260p.

A conference of representatives from various segments of the banking industry to discuss one of the major contemporary issues. Deals with the status of interstate banking legislation in Congress, the states and the courts, the strategies open to large and small banks, the effect of interstate banking on large bank-small bank competition, and the impact on the banking system and the public. The selected bibliography includes books, articles, published reports, government publications, conference proceedings and speeches.

85. Federal Reserve Bank of Atlanta. *Payments in the Financial Services Industry of the 1980's; Conference*

Proceedings. Westport, CT: Quorum, 1984.
203p.

Conference covers the types of products that
will lead to full-scale electronic financial service,
the problems that may be encountered in bank
and nonbank networks, the likely winners and
losers in the network race, the effects of regulation and of deregulation on the payments system,
the international implications, and future legislation.

86. Federal Reserve Bank of Atlanta. *Working Paper
    Series.* Atlanta, GA, 1976—.

    This series consists of theoretical studies on
    banking, and analyses of current developments
    and historical trends, especially for the sixth
    district. Each Federal Reserve Bank's papers also
    has a similar purpose and scope for its district.

87. Federal Reserve Bank of Boston. *Research Reports.*
    Boston, MA, 1958—.

88. Federal Reserve Bank of Chicago. *Proceedings of
    the Conference on Bank Structure and Competition.*
    Chicago, 1964—.

    Conferences held annually. Theme of the 23d
    conference held May 6–8, 1987, was the merging
    of commercial and investment banking. Other
    topics have been public policy toward failing
    thrift institutions, theory of financial intermedi-
    aries and the banking firm, bank lending deci-
    sions, interest rate swaps, bank equity markets,
    and results of recent studies of effects of market
    structure on performance in banking.

89. Federal Reserve Bank of Chicago. *Staff Memo-
    randa.* Chicago, 1967—.

90. Federal Reserve Bank of Cleveland. *Deregulation, Cost Cutting, and Competitive Pressures; Conference Proceedings, May 1, 1984.* Cleveland, OH, 1984. 49p.
    Examines the factors involved in operating a branch system, especially those to be considered in closing a branch.

91. Federal Reserve Bank of Cleveland. *Working Papers.* Cleveland, OH, 1976—.

92. Federal Reserve Bank of Dallas. *Research Papers.* Dallas, TX, 1978—.

93. Federal Reserve Bank of Kansas City. *Research Working Papers.* Kansas City, MO, 1977—.

94. Federal Reserve Bank of Kansas City. *Restructuring the Financial System.* Kansas City, MO, 1987. 243p.
    Papers from a symposium, held at Jackson Hole, WY, deal with the issues involved in financial reform and the various proposals for restructuring the financial system.

95. Federal Reserve Bank of New York. *Recent Trends in Commercial Bank Profitability. A Staff Study.* New York, 1986. 379p.
    Recent developments have given rise to concern whether our banking system can endure. This study by members of the New York Fed's staff in various departments is basically historical in nature to determine what has happened to bank profitability and why. The results of the study do not indicate a serious deterioration of the banking system, but certain trends are causes for concern.

96. Federal Reserve Bank of New York. *Research Papers.* New York, 1972—.

97. Federal Reserve Bank of Philadelphia. *Research Working Papers.* Philadelphia, PA, 1982—.

98. Federal Reserve Bank of Richmond. *Working Paper Series.* Richmond, VA, 1975—.

99. Federal Reserve Bank of St. Louis. *Research Papers.* St. Louis, MO, 1981—.

100. Federal Reserve Bank of San Francisco. *The Search for Financial Stability: The Past Fifty Years.* San Francisco, CA, 1985. 249p.

   Defining stability as the soundness of depository institutions in providing monetary assets, the papers of this conference compare bank failures in the 1930s and 1980s. Review the factors contributing to stability or instability. Examine the effects of supervision and regulation in ensuring financial stability.

101. Federal Reserve Bank of San Francisco. *Working Papers.* San Francisco, CA, 1971—.

102. Fischer, Gerald C. *The Modern Bank Holding Company: Development, Regulation, and Performance.* Philadelphia, PA: Temple University, 1986. 386p.

   This study, funded by the Association of Bank Holding Companies, is designed primarily as a reference book. Traces the general, regulatory and legislative history of BHCs (bank holding companies), their intrastate and interstate activities, and their effects on competition. There are two contributing authors, Joseph F. Sinkey, Jr. who wrote the chapter on safety and soundness of BHCs, and Robert A. Eisenbeis who wrote the chapters on BHC nonbank development and performance. There are an extensive bibliography and many footnotes.

103. Fraser, Donald R., and Kolari, James W. *The Future of Small Banks in a Deregulated Environment*. Cambridge, MA: Ballinger, 1985. 262p.

The small banks seem to be lost in the shuffle in the discussions of deregulation. Fraser and Kolari analyze the role of small banks in the United States financial system historically, the changes in regulations, the revolution in the banking and the financial services industry, and the effects of deregulation. They also discuss the strategic responses of small banks to deregulation and the new competition, and the implications for the future. Bibliography includes articles and monographs.

104. Frieden, Jeffry A. *Banking on the World: The Politics of American International Finance*. New York: Harper & Row, 1987. 264p.

Describes the development of American international banking and the impact of modern international banking on domestic and international economies and politics. Shows the conflicts arising over American international finance and the possible future outcome. There are chapter notes and a short bibliography.

105. Frieder, Larry A., et al. *Commercial Banking and Interstate Expansion: Issues, Prospects, and Strategies*. Research for Business Decisions, no. 74. Ann Arbor, MI: UMI Research Press, 1985. 181p.

Much of the contents of this book is the result of the Florida Interstate Banking Study commissioned by the Florida House of Representatives Committee on Commerce. However, the aim is to provide information to other states considering this issue. Studies the pros and cons of interstate banking as a whole, as well as the questions of the public interest and of the policies needed to achieve the best means of interstate banking. Includes bibliography and index.

106. Graddy, Duane B., ed. *The Bank Holding Company Performance Controversy.* Washington, DC: University Press of America, 1979. 807p.

A compilation of articles originally published in periodicals between 1971 and 1977. Theme is the growth of bank holding companies and the effect on their own performance, as well as the performance of the individual banks and the return on stockholders' investments. Discusses also the impact of bank holding companies on competition and the performance of their non-bank activities. Most articles contain references and bibliographies.

107. Gup, Benton E., ed. *Bank Mergers: Current Issues and Perspectives.* Boston, MA: Kluwer Academic Publishers, 1989, 135p.

Ten articles contributed by experts review the broad perspective of merger activity, analyze the effect of mergers on stockholders and discuss the regulatory concerns.

108. Havrilesky, Thomas M.; Schweitzer, Robert L.; and Boorman, John T., eds. *Dynamics of Banking.*

Arlington Heights, IL: Harlan Davidson, 1985. 447p.

Collection of readings on changes since 1980 caused by deregulation. Discusses bank management, financial innovation, accounts and profitability, constraints on geographical and product line expansion, international banking, and supervisory and regulatory reform.

109. Jessee, Michael A., and Seelig, Steven A. *Bank Holding Companies and the Public Interest: An Economic Analysis.* Lexington, MA: Lexington Books, 1977. 190p.

Directed to bankers, regulators and members of the academic community interested in the growth of bank holding companies, the regulation of that growth and its impact on public welfare. Deals with the development of bank holding companies, the effect on competition and on the efficiency of banking operation. Examines the impact of the bank holding company movement on the soundness and stability of the banking system and implications for public policy. There are chapter notes, as well as a bibliography.

110. Khoury, Sarkis J., and Ghosh, Alo, eds. *Recent Developments in International Banking and Finance.* Lexington, MA: Lexington Books, 1987 and 1988. Vols. 1 and 2.

Papers submitted to symposia sponsored by the University of California at Riverside in 1986 and 1987. Authors were practitioners and scholars in the field of international finance. Volume one develops the themes that internationalism is irreversible and international events affect the entire banking sector. That stability is impossi-

ble and can be realized in part only by competent and progressive management.

This management must be aware of the value of
information technology and maintain an updated database. Volume two deals with options,
third world debt, portfolio management, exchange rate forecasting and bank regulation.

111. Kim, Seung H., and Miller, Stephen W. *Competitive Structure of the International Banking Industry*.
Lexington, MA: Lexington Books, 1983. 234p.

A comparison of the financial and market
characteristics of major U.S. and foreign-bank-
ing competitors offering international banking
services in the U.S. Reviews the growth of
international business and of foreign banks in
the U.S. Describes the legislative environment
for international banking activities, the asset and
liability management structure, and the market
structure of international banking. Discusses
future trends in international banking.

112. Lawrence, Colin, and Shay, Robert P., eds.
*Technological Innovation, Regulation, and the Mon-
etary Economy*. Cambridge, MA: Ballinger, 1986.
222p.

A collection of revised papers, first delivered
at a conference held at the Graduate School of
Business, Columbia University, on March 15,
1985. The papers deal with the issues of how
technological change has affected the costs of
payment vehicles and the cost of supplying
financial services, the type and extent of regulation required by the new technology, and the
effect on monetary policy of greater speed in
transactions and communication.

113. Litan, Robert E. *What Should Banks Do?* Washington, DC: Brookings Institution, 1987. 207p.

    Examines current regulatory status of financial institutions and the range of their permissible activities. While the author does not foresee that federal barriers preventing banks and other organizations from competing in the same activities will be relaxed soon, he does predict that technological developments and deregulation at the state level will erode legal barriers, lead to diversification of product lines, and greater competition. Discusses the benefits and the risks of financial product diversification and the alternative routes banks can take to meet the challenges brought on by these changes.

114. Mayer, Martin. *The Money Bazaars: Understanding the Banking Revolution around Us.* New York: E. P. Dutton, 1984. 394p.

    A lively journalistic account of present-day banking. The author foresees the day when banking services are provided by a variety of institutions so that banking as an institution will no longer exist.

115. Nadler, Paul S. *Commercial Banking in the Economy.* 4th ed. New York: Random, 1986. 199p.

    For the general reader. Explains banking as a business, and the function of banks as intermediaries between Federal Reserve monetary policy and the economy. Shows how banks react to credit control in the allocation of bank assets and management of liabilities. Deals with the changing sources of bank deposits, the role of the thrifts, and the changes in the banking structure.

116. Pecchioli, R. M. *The Internationalisation of Banking: The Policy Issues*. Paris: Organization for Economic Cooperation and Development, 1983. 221p.

The first report of the inquiry into the banking structure and regulations in the OECD countries by the Committee on Financial Markets. Reviews the banks' international business, multinational banking, the foreign banking presence in OECD countries, the prudential control and supervision of banks' international business, and the microeconomic aspects. Annexes include the regulatory and supervisory activities of banks in various countries. Includes an extensive bibliography of articles and monographs.

117. Prochnow, Herbert V., ed. *The One-Bank Holding Company*. Graduate School of Banking, University of Wisconsin, Series in Economic Issues. Chicago: Rand McNally, 1969. 172p.

Early discussion by a number of leading academicians of the one-bank holding company movement. Covers the history of its development, and evaluates its present and likely future. Analyzes the Bank Holding Company Act of 1956 and its amendments of 1966, and looks to the pending legislation that passed in 1970.

118. Rose, Peter S. *The Changing Structure of American Banking*. New York: Columbia University Press, 1987. 419p.

A research study that deals with the developments in the banking industry since World War II and the impact upon the public. Examines the most important structural changes, such as size distribution of banks, concentration of banking resources, growth of new banks and holding companies and nonbank financial institutions. Reviews the concepts of the terms structure and organization. Discusses specific problem areas and the issues of regulation and deregulation. There are extensive references to journal articles and monographs at the end of each chapter.

119. Roussakis, Emmanuel N., ed. *International Banking; Principles and Practices.* New York: Praeger, 528p.

Designed for students, career individuals, academicians, lawyers, and customers of banks. Essays by the author and other contributors describe the function and structure of international banking, legal issues, risk and credit analysis, foreign loans and financing. Concluding section deals with the international role of U.S. banks, future trends in international banking, and the implications for regulation. There are suggested readings at the end of most chapters.

120. Sametz, Arnold W., ed. *Securities Activities of Commercial Banks.* Lexington, MA: Lexington Books, 1981. 191p.

Papers presented at a conference in 1979 at the Salomon Brothers Center for the Study of Financial Institutions of the Graduate School of Business Administration of New York University. Participants represented the banking and the securities industries, regulators and academicians. Concentrates on the state of the current controversy about banks' entry into securities activities. Explains and critically examines the current regulatory framework for banks' securities activities. Discusses the regulatory aspects of

new or expanding banks' securities activities.
Speculates about the future of expanded securities and other financing activities of banks and
securities firms.

121. U.S. Comptroller of the Currency. *Bank Failure:
An Evaluation of the Factors Contributing to the
Failure of National Banks.* Washington, DC, 1988.
34p.
    Study of selected national banks chosen from
among those that failed, those similarly situated
that experienced problems but recovered, and
those whose condition never deteriorated de-
spite problems in their local economies. Factors
contributing to healthy banks were sound management practices, an active board of directors,
realistic goals, good documentation and conser-
vative lending policies.

122. U.S. Congress. Senate. Committee on Banking,
Housing and Urban Affairs. *Compendium of
Issues Relating to Branching by Financial Institutions.* Washington, DC: Government Printing
Office, 1976. 521p.
    Papers and reports compiled for the Subcom-
mittee on Financial Institutions. The first five
are original articles surveying various aspects of
branching by banks and other financial institutions. The sixth and seventh articles were taken
from existing works and deal with off premise
electronic banking. Includes a review of the
literature. Several articles also have bibliographies.

123. U.S. General Accounting Office. *Banking: Con-
flict of Interest Abuses in Commercial Banking
Institutions.* Washington, DC, 1989. 72p.

Report to chairman, House Subcommittee on Commerce, Consumer, and Monetary Affairs. Defines the nature of conflicts of interest in the banking industry. Shows the current institutional conflicts of interest abuses and the factors controlling them. Discusses the potential conflicts and abuses that might arise if banking institutions are allowed to expand their securities powers. Report based on interviews with bankers and regulators, publications of trade associations and academic experts. Consensus is that competition, banking internal controls and regulatory oversight would help to keep conflicts in check.

124. U.S. President, 1977–1981 (Carter). *Geographic Restrictions on Commercial Banking in the United States; Report.* Washington, DC: Department of the Treasury, 1981. 234p.

Treats the issue whether the existing framework of geographical restrictions on bank expansion is an effective, efficient and equitable way to avoid undue concentration in the financial environment of the 1980s. Urges a phased liberalization of existing restraints as being in the best public interest. Appendix is a compendium of eight papers on branch banking prepared by the staffs of participating federal agencies.

125. Walter, Ingo, ed. *Deregulating Wall Street: Commercial Bank Penetration of the Corporate Securities Market.* New York: Wiley, 1985. 315p.

A collection of essays commissioned by J.P. Morgan & Co. in 1983 for a conference held at the Salomon Brothers Center for the Study of Financial Institutions. Addresses the questions,

"Was the Glass-Steagall Act warranted?" "Had
the nation gained or lost as a result?" and "What
are the economic implications of any deregulation?" Includes bibliographies.

126. Whitehead, David D. *A Guide to Interstate Banking*. Atlanta, GA: Federal Reserve Bank of
Atlanta, 1983. 121p.

Documents the extent to which banking
organizations provide bank-like service on an
interstate basis. Lists in detail the banking
organizations that provide such services by types
of service, where and by what subsidiaries.
Shows ways that bank holding companies provide interstate financial services, by organization
and by state.

5. INVESTMENT BANKING

127. Bloch, Ernest. *Inside Investment Banking.* 2d ed. Homewood, IL: Dow Jones-Irwin, 1989. 415p.

Written for the author's graduate seminar. Focuses on the market making function of investment firms and new issues finance. Emphasizes the innovative activities of investment bankers. The final part of the book discusses the institutionalization of the investment market. There is a glossary of common investment banking and financial terms, and suggestions for further readings.

128. Eccles, Robert G., and Crane, Dwight B. *Doing Deals: Investment Banks at Work.* Boston: Harvard Business School Press, 1988. 273p.

Based on 300 interviews concerning management practices in the investment banking industry. Illustrates what the industry is all about by describing the deals First Boston Corporation did for Union Carbide. Authors use the case of Union Carbide to illustrate their management theory. Recent trend of shift from single to multiple investment bank relationships by issuing customers has affected management strategies. Strategies are developed at the grass roots level and are flexible and dependent on a system of networks in the industry that strengthens the managerial process. Authors discuss the implications of their theory for the future when commercial banks enter the investment banking field and when other types of organizations acquire investment banks. Bibliography includes articles and books.

129. Friend, Irwin, et al. *Investment Banking and the New Issues Market.* Cleveland, OH: World, 1967. 598p.

      This study, made by the Securities Research Unit of the Wharton School of Finance and Commerce at the University of Pennsylvania under a grant from the Investment Bankers Association, focuses on data for the first quarter of 1962 supplied by the industry. Emphasizes corporate and municipal new issues. Reviews and describes the function and operation of the investment banking industry. Although focus is on first quarter of 1962, the analyses are placed in historical perspective. Bibliographic footnotes.

130. Hayes, Samuel L., III; Spence, A. Michael; and Marks, David VanPraag. *Competition in the Investment Banking Industry.* Cambridge, MA: Harvard University Press, 1983. 177p.

      Traces the history of competition in the investment banking field and the trends toward concentration. Analyzes the current situation by showing the major investment banks and their client base and the process of matching banks and clients. Illustrated by tables. Includes notes.

131. Hoffman, Paul. *The Dealmakers: Inside the World of Investment Banking.* Garden City, NY: Doubleday, 1984. 238p.

      Well-known journalist describes investment banks and bankers, and how they conduct their business. A nontechnical work that serves as an introduction for the layperson.

132. Perez, Robert C. *Inside Investment Banking.* New York: Praeger, 1984. 203p.

     Discusses investment banking's function in providing venture capital for new industries. Chapters deal with the originating and marketing functions, syndicated offerings, private placement, mergers and acquisitions, the types of securities offered, the dealer and buyers, and finally, some reflections on the challenges and controversies facing the industry today. There is an extensive bibliography.

133. Williamson, J. Peter, ed. *Investment Banking Handbook.* New York: Wiley, 1988. 574p.

     Experienced investment bankers and observers contribute chapters on how the investment industry operates and where its future lies. Topics include raising capital, transactional activities, specialized financial instruments, tax-exempt financing, commercial banks and investment banking, investment banking outside the United States. Lists the 75 leading managers and underwriters.

134. Willis, Henry Parker, and Bogen, Jules I. *Investment Banking.* rev. ed. New York: Harper, 1936. 667p.

     Early text still useful for fundamental information and history of investment banking.

6. SAVINGS INSTITUTIONS

135. Balderston, Frederick E. *Thrifts in Crisis: Structural Transformation of the Savings and Loan Industry.* Cambridge, MA: Ballinger, 1985. 191p.

A study of the changes in the structure of the savings and loan industry, and their public policy implications. Analyzes the large size of mortgage portfolio discount of the S&L industry, the merger activity between 1980 and 1982, and the new entries into the industry. Aims to provide a series of guidelines for the regulators and for the executives confronting new problems of the survival of their firms. References at the end of each chapter.

136. Bergengren, Roy F.; Gartland, Agnes C.; and Brown, James W. *Crusade: The Fight for Economic Democracy in North America, 1921–1945.* New York: Exposition, 1952. 379p.

Bergengren was a leader in the cooperative banking movement in the United States. He headed the Filene-financed Credit Union National Extension Bureau and oversaw its conversion to the present Credit Union National Association. This book relates the credit union movement and Bergengren's efforts to secure suitable state and federal laws to make it possible. Chapter two, written by James W. Brown, "What Is a Credit Union?" is an excellent introduction to this aspect of banking.

137. Brumbaugh, R. Dan, Jr. *Thrifts under Siege: Restoring Order to American Banking.* Cambridge, MA: Ballinger, 1988. 214p.

    Analyzes the economic forces causing upheaval in the banking industry. Uses the thrift industry to illustrate the need for dramatic reform in bank regulation. Reviews the origin and growth of thrifts and how they suffered the crises of 1980 and 1987 and the effects of regulatory action. Describes the steps that must be taken to close insolvent thrifts at minimum cost. Argues for a rise in required minimum net worth on capital for remaining institutions and better monitoring. Makes a case for consolidating the regulatory agencies.

138. Carron, Andrew S. *The Plight of the Thrift Institutions.* Washington, DC: Brookings Institution, 1982. 96p.

    Reviews the state of the thrift industry and the outlook for its future under various economic assumptions. Discusses the role that government agencies must play in supporting the thrifts in the transition to deregulation. Makes recommendations for more efficient use of government resources, mergers and services.

139. Dublin, Jack. *Credit Unions: Theory and Practice.* 2d ed. Detroit, MI: Wayne State University, 1971. 186p.

    Written as a result of the author's assignment in Tanganyika (now Tanzania). Purpose is to help people, especially in third world countries, and their governments to start a credit union movement. Presents the basic philosophy of the credit union movement and how it is applied.

Useful as a primer on credit unions. Contains a bibliography.

140. Ewalt, Josephine Hedges. *A Business Reborn: The Savings and Loan Story, 1930–1960.* Chicago: American Saving and Loan Institution Press, 1962. 406p.

A survey of the savings and loan industry beginning with the legislation of the 30s, the establishment of the Federal Home Loan Bank System and the insurance of S&L accounts. The story continues with the effect of World War II and the post-war developments. Appendix 2 is a synopsis of two previous studies, *History of Building & Loan in the United States* by Morton Bodfish and *As It Was in the Beginning*, a commemoration of the first 125 years of the industry.

141. Federal Home Loan Bank of San Francisco. *Thrift Performance and Capital Adequacy.* Proceedings of the Twelfth Annual Conference. San Francisco, CA, 1987. 187p.

Fifteen papers, presented by thrift and banking regulators, Wall Street and West Coast financial consultants. Sessions discussed the pros and cons of capital requirements, competitive intermediation, off-balance sheet activity and profitability, and coping with regulatory net worth requirements. Previous conferences concerned the structure, management, regulation and financial stability of the savings and loan industry.

142. Federal Reserve Bank of Boston. *The Future of the Thrift Industry; Proceedings.* Boston, 1982. 87p.

Surveys the condition of the Massachusetts

savings banks and the California savings and loan associations. Describes the Canadian experience with thrift institutions and compares the European housing finance systems. Suggests short-run financial and structural solutions to the problems of the U.S. thrift institutions, and projects the future role of thrifts in mortgage lending.

143. Friend, Irwin. *Study of the Savings and Loan Industry. Submitted to the Federal Home Loan Bank Board.* Washington, DC: Government Printing Office, 1969. 4 vols.

Study authorized by Congress in 1966 to examine the role of the savings and loan industry in the economy, and to determine methods for improving its performance. Twenty major papers, which are either fact finding or policy oriented, represent the most comprehensive analysis of the S&L industry up to that time. The first volume synthesizes the findings of the papers and lists the more important recommendations for legislative and regulatory action.

144. Gart, Alan. *Banks, Thrifts and Insurance Companies: Surviving the 1980's.* Lexington, MA: Lexington Books, 1985. 136p.

Designed to help those in the financial services industry to cope with the changes in the financial industry brought about by deregulation and the rapid developments in technology.

145. Interagency Task Force on Thrift Institutions. *Report.* Washington, DC: U.S. Senate. Committee on Banking, Housing and Urban Affairs, 1980. 267p.

Submitted to Congress at the direction of the
Depository Institutions Deregulation and Monetary Control Act of 1980 by the task force,
composed of members of the regulatory agencies and several departments of the government. The report analyzes the problems faced
by the thrift institutions, and examines various
options available to provide balance to the
asset-liability management problem; to increase
the ability of thrift institutions to pay market
rates of interest in periods of inflation; and
through federal agencies to assist thrifts in times
of economic difficulties.

146. Knight, Henry, and Peasgood, Wayne. *Credit
Union Performance Improvement: Practical Ideas for
Directors and Managers.* Chicago: Probus, 1989.
388p.
Co-sponsored by Coopers & Lybrand and
Credit Union Executive Society. Examines the
need to improve performance, how to evaluate
a credit union's position, performance and
prospects, how to implement improvements,
and fine-tuning for excellence.

147. Melvin, Donald J.; Davis, Raymond N.; and
Fischer, Gerald C. *Credit Unions and the Credit
Union Industry; a Study of the Powers, Organiza-
tions, Regulation and Competition.* New York: New
York Institute of Finance, 1977. 321p.
A comprehensive source of information on
credit unions and the credit union industry.
Reviews the organization, powers and character-
istics of CUs; government regulation; and the
political and market structure of the industry.
Discusses the industry's problems and prospects,
especially in competing with other depository

institutions, and the impact of electronic funds transfer.

148. Moody, J. Carroll, and Fite, Gilbert C. *The Credit Union Movement: Origins and Development 1850–1980.* 2d ed. Dubuque, IA: Kendall/Hunt, 1984. 354p.

A history of the institutional growth of credit unions. Analyzes the credit union movement from a social point of view. A bibliographic note discusses the sources of information on credit unions.

149. Ornstein, Franklin H. *Savings Banking: an Industry in Change.* Reston, VA: Reston Publishing Co., 1985. 350p.

A good general history of savings banking, published for the Bank Administration Institute. Describes the function of savings institutions, their operation and management. Discusses the regulatory changes of the legislation of 1980 and 1982. The bibliography includes books and articles.

150. Pugh, Olive S., and Ingram, F. Jury. *Credit Unions: A Movement Becomes an Industry.* Reston, VA: Reston Publishing Co., 1984. 229p.

Traces the maturation of the credit union movement from small, somewhat informal savings type of organizations to the well-organized and larger financial institutions of today. Deals with the early history, organization and industry structure, regulation and management, economics and position in the financial market place, and the future of the industry. Includes discussion of major legislation including the

Garn-St Germain Depository Institutions Act of
1982. References are to books as well as articles.

151. Woerheide, Walter J. *The Savings and Loan
Industry: Current Problems and Possible Solutions.*
Westport, CT: Quorum, 1984. 216p.

Examines the present state of the savings and
loan industry and how it developed. Reviews the
efforts being made to return S&Ls to a profita-
ble industry. Gives a historical overview. Discusses profitability measures, new services,
mergers, conversions, and the outlook for the
future. There are notes at the end of each
chapter and a bibliography.

7. LAW AND REGULATION

152. Auerbach, Joseph, and Hayes, Samuel L., III. *Investment Banking and Diligence: What Price Deregulation?* Boston: Harvard Business School Press, 1986. 274p.

    A fairly technical discussion of the regulation of investment banking. Gives a historical overview of fifty years of regulatory experience. Then focuses on the recent regulatory change of Rule 415 of the Securities and Exchange Commission, which allows corporations to file a single S-3 "shelf registration" statement, discusses the implications of this rule, especially as it affects the tradition of diligence: guarding against hasty new issues. There are examples of use of shelf registration and the authors' recommendation for future public policy. Appendix I shows an agreement among underwriters and Appendix II gives a sample prospectus. There is a glossary.

153. Benston, George J., et al. *Perspectives on Safe Banking: Past, Present, & Future.* Cambridge, MA: MIT Press, 1986. 358p.

    Commissioned by the American Bankers Association, five leading academicians studied the issues surrounding the safety and soundness of the banking industry and the efficacy of the regulatory system. The authors' conclusions are that as long as the regulatory agencies do their job, the banking system will remain sound; Congress should tread a wary path between complete deregulation and reregulation; the federal insurance instruments should be strengthened; and there needs to be more information on market value of banks' assets and liabilities in order for investors and depositors to make decisions.

154. Benton, Donald S., and Douglas, James A., eds. *Federal Banking Laws.* 3d ed. Boston: Warren, Gorham & Lamont, 1987. v.p.

   Focuses on commercial and retail banking as covered in sections of Title 12 of the U.S. Code and some other sections. Illustrated by cases. Cumulative supplements will be published periodically.

155. Beutel, Frederick K., and Schroeder, Milton R. *Bank Officer's Handbook of Commercial Banking Law.* 5th ed. Boston: Warren, Gorham & Lamont, 1982. 590p. Cumulative supplement No. 2, 1987.

   Reviews the nature and regulation of banking. Discusses commercial paper, duties of banks and customers. Describes special transactions and bankruptcy, and special consumer credit regulation. Includes a table of cases and index.

156. Chamness, Robert P. *The Garn-St Germain Depository Institutions Act of 1982: A Complete Reference for Bankers.* Rolling Meadows, IL: Bank Administration Institute, 1983. v.p.

   A thorough explanation of the provisions of the Act and its effects on the banking industry. Gives the history, background, overview and analysis of the Act. Details the bank-related provisions, real estate-related provisions, provisions pertaining to other financial institutions, and provisions on failing or troubled institutions. Each part contains regulatory reference material. Includes texts of statutes.

157. Clark, Barkley. *The Law of Bank Deposits, Collections and Credit Cards.* Rev. ed. Boston: Warren, Gorham & Lamont, 1981. v.p. Cumulative supplement No. 3, 1987.

Based primarily upon Articles 4 and 5 of the Uniform Commercial Code and the Federal Truth-in-Lending Act. Includes all significant cases pertaining to the laws concerning bank deposits, collections and credit cards. Explores the relationship between drawer and holder, and discusses the competition for funds in the drawer account. Describes the laws and rules relating to the bank check, forgery, documentary draft, letters of credit, credit cards and bank set off. Explores the legal framework which might apply as we move toward a checkless society. Applies to savings and loan and credit union institutions, as well as commercial banks. Appendix includes texts and official comments on the pertinent UCC articles.

158. Conboy, James C., Jr. *Law & Banking—Principles.* 2d ed. Washington, DC: American Bankers Association, 1986. 295p.

An introduction to the legal aspects of banking. Discusses bank regulation and describes the function of the Comptroller of the Currency, Federal Reserve Board, FDIC and state banking authorities. Deals with torts and crimes, legal entities, contracts, real and personal property,

bankruptcy, and the legal implications of consumer lending. Includes glossary of legal terms
related to banking and commercial transactions.
A handy desk reference with its companion
volume by Craig W. Smith.

159. Cooper, Kerry, and Fraser, Donald R. *Banking
Deregulation and the New Competition in Financial
Services.* Cambridge, MA: Ballinger, 1984. 278p.

A comprehensive study of the regulation of
depository institutions. Examines the original
rationale of financial regulation both from a
domestic and international point of view, and
shows how the changes and innovations in the
financial services industry will affect competition. One chapter is devoted to the Depository
Institutions Deregulation and Monetary Control Act of 1980 and includes tables showing
proposals and final adoption, milestones in
deregulation and a table of major provisions.
Another chapter describes the Garn-St Germain
Depository Institutions Act of 1982. There are
notes at the end of each chapter and an
extensive bibliography mostly of journal articles.

160. Dale, Richard. *The Regulation of International
Banking.* Englewood Cliffs, NJ: Prentice-Hall,
1986. 208p.

Describes the growth of multinational banking and the need for a formal framework of
international law for its regulation. Chapters
deal with international banking risks, preventa-
tive regulation and protective regulation, and
international supervisory cooperation.

161. Edwards, Franklin R., ed. *Issues in Financial
Regulation.* New York: McGraw-Hill, 1979. 526p.

Papers, comments and discussion are an outgrowth of a series of faculty seminars held 1976–1977 at the Columbia University Center for Law and Economic Studies. Presents views of legal and economic scholars on the effects of regulation on banking structure and soundness, on the credit markets, and on multinational banking, as well as the implication of an electronic funds transfer system. Includes bibliography.

162. England, Catherine, and Huertas, Thomas, eds. *The Financial Services Revolution: Policy Directions for the Future.* Boston: Kluwer, 1988. 361p.

Fifth in a series of annual conferences sponsored by Cato Institute in 1987 to examine public policy toward the monetary and banking system. Focuses on regulation of depository institutions. Examines the questions of bank ownership, activities of banks' affiliates and the regulation and supervision of banks.

163. Federal Deposit Insurance Corporation. *Deposit Insurance in a Changing Environment: A Study of the Current System of Deposit Insurance Pursuant to Sect. 712 of the Garn-St Germain Depository Institutions Act of 1982; Submitted to Congress.* Washington, DC, 1983. 1 vol., v.p.

Objectives of the study were to seek ways to impose a greater degree of marketplace discipline on the deposit insurance system in order to replace outmoded government controls; and to seek ways to assure that in a deregulated environment the regulatory and insurance systems are as effective, efficient and equitable as possible. Report consists of twelve articles by different contributors covering all aspects of deposit insurance existing and proposed. Two chapters review the literature on risk related insurance systems for commercial banks and on failure prediction models for commercial banks. There are additional bibliographies. One of three reports to Congress mandated by the Garn-St Germain Act. See also Federal Home Loan Bank Board, *Agenda for Reform,* and National Credit Union Administration, *Credit Union Share Insurance.*

164. Federal Deposit Insurance Corporation. *Federal Deposit Insurance Corporation, the First Fifty Years: a History of the FDIC 1933–1983.* Washington, DC, 1984. 148p.

  Written to commemorate the FDIC's fiftieth birthday, this small book gives a concise treatment of the institutional antecedents and the developments of deposit insurance since 1933. Deals with the legislation concerning the FDIC and its operations and activities. Contains a bibliography of books and articles.

165. Federal Home Loan Bank Board. *Agenda for Reform: A Report on Deposit Insurance to the Congress.* Washington, DC, 1983. 416p.

  One of three reports prepared pursuant to the Garn-St Germain Depository Institutions Act of 1982. Focuses on the system of deposit insurance and its impact on the structure and operation of depository institutions. Examines various options for revision and makes recommendations. Includes references and bibliography. This report, along with the ones prepared by the Federal Deposit Insurance Corporation and the National Credit Union Administration, also published for the use of both houses of

Congress under the title of *Report to Congress on Federal Deposit Insurance.*

166. Federal Reserve Bank of Chicago. *Leveling the Playing Field: A Review of the DIDMCA of 1980 and the Garn-St Germain Act of 1982.* Readings in Economics and Finance. Chicago, 1983. 55p.

    Articles originally published in the Bank's *Economic Perspectives.* First section presents a title-by-title description of the Depository Institutions Deregulation and Monetary Control Act of 1980. Additional articles discuss the history and major provisions of the Garn-St Germain Act of 1982, its impact on S&Ls, commercial banks and bank holding companies, the implications for monetary policy and what remains to be done. Includes references.

167. Fischer, L. Richard; Gentry, Elizabeth G.; and Verderamo, Petrina M. E. *The Garn-St Germain Depository Institutions Act of 1982: What's in It for You.* Arlington, VA: The Consumer Bankers Association, 1982. 143p.

    Legislative history of the Act and a title-by-title analysis of its provisions. Emphasizes the Act's effect on commercial banks. Also includes a discussion of the Export Trading Company Act of 1982 which gives banks authority to invest in export trading companies. A sixteen page supplement, published in 1982, discusses the money market deposit account and the "Super-NOW" accounts, as provided by section 327 of the Act.

168. Gart, Alan. *The Insiders Guide to the Financial Services Revolution.* New York: McGraw-Hill, 1986. 198p.

The revolution is the one brought about by changes in technology, distribution systems and deregulation. Describes the effect of the changes on the financial services industry, including brokers, commercial and investment banks, thrifts, money market funds, and insurance companies. Assesses the implications of increased competition and the probable future developments. Includes recommended strategies for small and large banks, thrifts and other financial intermediaries, and for employees at financial institutions for investments and personal finance. Includes notes at the end of each chapter.

169. Goldberg, Lawrence G., and White, Lawrence J., eds. *The Deregulation of the Banking and Securities Industries.* Lexington, MA: Heath, 1979. 356p.

Papers presented at a conference sponsored by the Salomon Brothers Center for the Study of Financial Institutions, Graduate School of Business, New York University, held in May 1978. Participants consisted of the regulated, the regulators and interested outside parties. Reviews the status of regulation and deregulation in the banking and securities industries. Discusses developments in the securities industry and in the banking industry. Examines the intersection of the two industries. There are notes and references at the end of each paper and comments from people in the field. Even though the conference took place before the new legislation, it is an excellent discussion of the climate and the issues that gave rise to the deregulation legislation.

170. Golembe, Carter H., and Holland, David S. *Federal Regulation of Banking, 1986/87*. Washington, DC: Golembe Associates, 1986. 333p.

      The earlier editions, beginning in 1975, were published by the American Institute of Bankers and the American Bankers Association, and concerned primarily the commercial banks. This edition gives equal treatment to savings and loans, savings banks and credit unions. Begins with a brief historical review of regulation. Continues with a description of regulation of every aspect of banking including the international arena. Discusses the future of federal bank regulation. Includes an extensive statistical section, a listing of major banking laws, 1863 to 1983, a chronological listing of court cases mentioned in the text, and a selected bibliography.

171. Golembe Associates. *Commercial Banking and the Glass-Steagall Act*. Washington, DC: American Bankers Association, 1982. 148p.

      Concerned with the four sections of the Banking Act of 1933 on the securities industry and the commercial banking industry. These sections prepared by Glass and Steagall gave the name to the whole Act. This study gives a historical overview of the relationship between commercial banking and the securities business. Describes the way the Act separates the two businesses. Discusses the present relevance of the Act. Presents the case for a new law and new approaches to regulation.

172. Heller, Pauline B. *Federal Bank Holding Company Law*. New York: Law Journal Seminars-Press, 1988. Looseleaf.

Defines a bank holding company. Reviews the company expansion of bank interests and non-bank interests that require and those that do not require Federal Reserve Board approval. Describes the handling of divestiture and procedures to follow in complying with the bank holding company laws. Updated periodically.

173. Kaufman, George G., and Kormendi, Roger C., eds. *Deregulating Financial Services: Public Policy in Flux*. Cambridge, MA: Ballinger, 1986. 223p.

Seven contributed essays, six of which were originally presented at the Mid American Institute for Public Policy Research in 1985. The seventh paper by George J. Benston was originally published in the *Journal of Bank Research*. It presents a historical overview of government regulation. The other essays were designed as basis for discussion by leading officials of a broad range of financial institutions, federal and state regulators and academic experts on the implications of continuing changes in the financial services industry and for constructing an agenda for public policy responses. Concludes with the Institute's report and recommendations, with dissenting views. One of the results of the symposium was the organization of a shadow Regulatory Commission in 1986. There are references at the end of each chapter.

174. Lash, Nicholas A. *Banking Laws and Regulations: An Economic Perspective*. Englewood Cliffs, NJ: Prentice-Hall, 1987. 200p.

A guide for bankers and observers of banking, also useful as a text. Places banking laws and regulations in historical perspective and evaluates their effect on the present economic environment. Presents the goals and purposes of banking regulations and describes the regulatory agencies. Treats balance sheet regulation and bank safety. Deals with special topics, such as investment banking, insurance activities and bank trusts, as well as off-balance sheet items, the U.S. payments system and international banking. Includes bibliography.

175. Littlewood, Shain & Company. *The Depository Institutions Deregulation and Monetary Control Act of 1980: An Analysis and Interpretation.* Park Ridge, IL: Bank Administration Institute, 1981. 160p.

A practical guide for the banker on the provisions and implications of the Act and its effects on bank operations.

176. National Credit Union Administration. *Credit Union Share Insurance: A Report to Congress.* Washington, DC, 1983. 76p.

One of three studies mandated by the Garn-St Germain Act. Report, based primarily on letters and comments from credit union leaders, state regulators, private insurance corporations, and credit union trade associations, discusses the impact of insurance on credit unions, the feasibility and effect of expanding insurance coverage, deposit insurance premiums risk factors, public disclosure practices and feasibility of consolidating the three federal deposit insurance funds. The other reports were prepared by the FDIC and the FHLBB.

177. Pecchioli, R. M. *Prudential Supervision in Banking.* Paris: Organization for Economic Cooperation and Development, 1987. 298p.

Part of the series on trends in banking structure and regulation in OECD countries. Surveys the main policy issues being met by OECD member countries as the result of market and technical changes affecting the structure of the banking system. Shows the efforts to preserve the integrity of the financial system in the face of these changes. The annexes describe specific regulations country by country. There are chapter notes and a bibliography.

178. Pitt, Harvey L.; Miles, David M.; and Ain, Anthony. *The Law of Financial Services.* Clifton, NJ: Prentice Hall Law & Business, 1988. 6 vols.

Describes the legal framework governing product expansion in the financial services industry as defined in the various acts, especially the Glass-Steagall Act, and explains the new exceptions made in the recent legislation. Discusses the federal and state laws governing interstate banking, and the recent federal legislative developments affecting geographical expansion of financial services. Appendixes list statutes, unpublished judicial decisions, laws and regulations of the Comptroller of the Currency, Board of Governors of the Federal Reserve System, Federal Deposit Insurance Corporation, Federal Home Loan Bank Board and Securities and Exchange Commission. There are tables of cases, statutes and regulations. Includes bibliography at the end of each chapter.

179. Pollard, Alfred M., et al. *Banking Law in the United States.* Stoneham, MA: Butterworth, 1988. 750p.

A guide to legislative, regulatory and court

actions covering every major area of banking regulation. Provides up-to-date information as well as historical background. Plans are to update this volume as required.

180. Saunders, Anthony, and White, Lawrence J., eds. *Technology and the Regulation of Financial Markets: Securities, Futures, and Banking.* Lexington, MA: Heath, 1986. 193p.

Papers are an outgrowth of a conference held by Salomon Brothers Center for the Study of Financial Institutions in 1985. Technological change has allowed the creation of new financial services and transactions and has led to innovative measures to bypass certain regulations. The authors examine how technological change has affected the corporate securities market, the futures markets and the banking industry. They discuss the increased risks in banks' daily transactions and portfolios, and the ways to combat them.

181. Smith, Craig W. *Law & Banking—Applications.* 2d ed. Washington, DC: American Bankers Association, 1986. 182p.

Designed to be used in conjunction with the volume written by James Conboy, this volume deals with the laws pertaining to secured transactions, letters of credit, and the bank collection process. Chapters are illustrated by cases related to banking practices. There is a glossary.

182. Spong, Kenneth. *Banking Regulation: Its Purposes, Implementation and Effects.* 2d ed. Kansas City, MO: Federal Reserve Bank of Kansas City, 1985. 173p.

Written as a text for the Graduate School of

Banking at Colorado, discusses the regulatory framework and recent significant changes in banking. Reviews the history and reason for regulating banks. Describes banks, bank holding companies and the regulatory agencies. Shows the advantages of regulation. Discusses future trends.

183. Task Group on Regulation of Financial Services. *Blueprint for Reform.* Washington, DC: Government Printing Office, 1984. 120p.

The committee, chaired by Vice-President Bush, reviewed the federal financial regulatory system with the goal to develop practical proposals to strengthen the effectiveness of federal regulation, while also encouraging competition and reducing unnecessary costs. The report makes more than four dozen recommendations affecting the thrift and commercial banking systems, and the deposit insurance system, and concerning the allocation of federal and state regulatory activities, streamlining of unnecessary regulatory controls and equality of competition.

184. U.S. Congress. House. Committee on Banking, Finance and Urban Affairs. *Compilation of Selected Banking Laws; Revised through January 1, 1984.* Washington, DC: Government Printing Office, 1984. 463p.

Texts of the major banking laws, beginning with the Federal Reserve Act, 1913. Includes subject index.

185. U.S. Congress. House. Committee on Banking, Finance and Urban Affairs. *Reference Guide to*

Banking and Finance. 2d rev. ed. Washington, DC: Government Printing Office, 1983. 102p.

Prepared by the Congressional Research Service, contains a glossary of terms and organizations and a bibliography related to banking and finance; and summaries of significant federal, banking (beginning with the National Bank Act of 1863), housing and securities laws.

186. U.S. Congress. Senate. Committee on Banking and Currency. *Federal Banking Laws and Reports: A Compilation of Major Federal Banking Documents, 1780–1912.* Washington, DC: Government Printing Office, 1963. 529p.

Compiled on the occasion of the Senate Banking Committee's fiftieth anniversary, brings together a number of major federal banking statutes enacted from the beginning of the republic.

187. U.S. Congress. Senate. Committee on Banking, Housing and Urban Affairs. *Compendium of Major Issues in Bank Regulation.* Washington, DC, 1975. 1089p.

Articles prepared by nongovernmental banking experts at the Committee's request on bank regulation and reform.

8. BANK MANAGEMENT

188. American Bankers Association. *Financial Planning for Bankers*. Washington, DC, 1985. 302p.

    Written by a team of experts to present bankers with a basic overview of financial planning and to make them aware of ways to apply financial planning to expanded customer services. Includes a short bibliography and glossary.

189. American Institute of Certified Public Accountants. *Audits of Banks: Prepared by the Banking Committee; Including the Accounting Standards*. 2d ed. New York, 1984. 198p.

    Designed for use by independent CPAs who audit banks. A practical guide presenting typical audit situations found in banks. Includes references to AICPA Statements on Auditing Standards and the authoritative pronouncements of the Financial Accounting Standards Board through November 1, 1982. Since changes in accounting standards are continually being made by the Accounting Standards Executive Committee, and new opinions are rendered by the FASB, this book serves only as an overview of generally accepted accounting practices and should not be used as a guide without reference to later changes in rules of accounting practices.

190. Arthur Andersen & Co., and Bank Administration Institute. *New Dimensions in Banking: Man-*

aging the Strategic Position. Park Ridge, IL: Bank Administration Institute, 1983. 54p.

Result of a Delphi study survey among industry experts to forecast the future strategies most likely to achieve success in bank management. Covers future trends in regulation, industry structures, technology, bank financial performance, bank sources and use of funds, market outlooks and strategies, and strategic planning.

191. Aspinwall, Richard, and Eisenbeis, Robert A., eds. *Handbook for Banking Strategy.* New York: Wiley, 1985. 800p.

Provides a good background of the current situation in banking; and reviews the effects on the financial services industry of the economic, political and market developments between 1975 and 1984. Essays, contributed by twenty-seven experts, deal with the role of intermediaries in fostering economic activity, the major forces for change affecting financial intermediation, the manifestations of banking change, and the major challenges to effective management.

192. Association of Reserve City Bankers, and Arthur Andersen & Co. *Strategic Issues in Banking.* Washington, DC, 1985. 66p.

A survey conducted by Arthur Andersen & Co. of ARCB members to determine their plans, opinions and assumptions about regulation, expansion and acquisition strategies. Other sections include opportunities in technology, competitive strategies, profitability of market segments and profit improvement opportunities. Also includes a market survey of 100 consumers with annual incomes exceeding $35,000; and a market survey of 100 chief financial officers of companies with sales ranging from $50 million to $100 million. Designed to serve as a planning tool for marketing banking services to the 1990s.

193. Asson, Thomas H., and Jones, Seymour. *The Bankers Guide to Audit Reports and Financial Statements.* Boston: Warren, Gorham & Lamont, 1979. 80p.

A guide for the banker explains the auditor's function, responsiblities and the standards and procedures that are followed. Shows the auditor's report and explains line by line how to interpret it. Illustrates the standard short form and variations of the report. Explains the significance of the financial statements. Gives a short list of selected readings to help in interpreting and analyzing financial statements. Describes other reports. Includes an illustrative study of a hypothetical company. The appendixes serve as indexes to the main sections of the study.

194. Austin, Douglas V., and Mandula, Mark S. *Banker's Handbook for Strategic Planning; How to Develop and Implement a Successful Strategy.* Boston: Bankers Publishing Co., 1985. 195p.

A "how to" book to aid bank managers and boards of directors to perform strategic planning. Describes the changing financial environment and the role of strategic planning. Gives a step-by-step analysis of the strategic planning process. The bibliography includes mainly periodical articles.

195. Austin, Douglas V.; Hokala, Donald R.; and Scampini, Thomas J. *Modern Banking; a Practical Guide to Managing Deregulated Financial Institutions.* Boston: Bankers Publishing Co., 1985. 406p.

Written for managers and executives in all types of financial institutions. Arranged by topic rather than institution. Discusses environmental factors that are changing the functions of banks and other depository institutions, the increasing role of the financial services firm, the impact of monetary policy on management of financial institutions, and the effects of supervisory and regulatory changes. Explains how to obtain and retain resources, asset and liability planning, and the management of operational functions. The guide is detailed and timely. There are brief notes at the end of most chapters.

196. Ballarin, Eduard. *Commercial Banks Amid the Financial Revolution: Developing a Competitive Strategy.* Cambridge, MA: Ballinger, 1986. 248p.

A historical and analytical approach to the structural revolution that is taking place in the financial services industry and the important issues facing commercial banks today. Discusses the strategies needed by banks to meet increased competition due to changes brought about by deregulation, information technology, and financial innovation. There is a short bibliography.

197. Baughn, William H.; Storrs, Thomas I.; and Walker, Charls E., eds. *The Bankers' Handbook.* 3d ed. Homewood, IL: Dow Jones-Irwin, 1988. 1347p.

Standard reference for students and those concerned with banking. Written by a panel of authors, essays deal with those subjects most important to performance in banking. Describes banking in the overall financial structure. Discusses the management of finances, the bank's credit services, and human resources. Reviews retail and wholesale banking, and trust services. Discusses bank supervision and regulation, and the impact of monetary and fiscal policies on the banking system.

198. Baughn, William H., and Mandich, Donald R., eds. *The International Banking Handbook.* Homewood, IL: Dow Jones-Irwin, 1983. 853p.

Essays, contributed by practitioners and professors, concern the major issues and functions involved in international banking. Introductory section describes the international financial system, markets, international banking in the U.S., and the role played by U.S. banks. Subsequent sections detail the operation and services of international banking.

199. Blackstone, William J., et al. *Bank Control and Audit.* Washington, DC: American Bankers Association, 1983. 296p.

Written for nonauditors to introduce them to the principles of auditing and the relationship between the bank's auditing function and the goals and objectives of the bank. Introduces the philosophy underlying the internal audit. Relates audit practice to specific bank activities, and illustrates additional approaches to bank auditing within the bank environment.

200. Brauns, Robert A. W., Jr., and Slater, Sarah W., eds. *Bankers Desk Reference*. Boston: Warren, Gorham & Lamont, 1978. 670p.

    Comprehensive handbook for bankers, treasurers and professionals who deal with the financial industry. Articles written by experts describe all aspects of banking operation: deposits, consumer credit, commercial lending, funds management, bank supervision and regulation, bank holding companies, international banking, and the mathematics of banking. There are notes at the end of each chapter, and a glossary.

201. Cambridge Research Institute. *Trends Affecting the U.S. Banking System*. Cambridge MA: Ballinger, 1976. 206p.

    A report on the current situation in the banking industry to give managers an analytical framework with which to plan strategies for developing new products and acquisitions relating to banking. Shows the relationship of the banking industry to its changing environment: economic, competitive, regulatory and technological. Draws conclusions on the future position of banks in the financial system, the shortage of funds, and the regulatory picture. There is an extensive bibliography.

202. Channon, Derek F. *Bank Strategic Management and Marketing*. New York: Wiley, 1986. 246p.

    This book and its accompanying case book are a development of the International Banking Center at the Manchester Business School and from work undertaken with many individual banks. Designed as an introduction to strategic planning for officers and trainees, it focuses on the marketing strategies needed to meet the changes faced by banks as the industry becomes more international.

203. Cole, Leonard P. *Management Accounting in Banks, for Executive Information and Control Reporting*. Rolling Meadows, IL: Bank Administration Institute, 1988. 225p.

Designed for bank executives and directors accountable for the performance of a bank, but with little time to learn, and for CFOs, controllers and management accountants directly responsible for the operation of a bank. Discusses strategic planning, tactical planning and budgeting, management information reporting systems, cost and profitability reporting and asset liability management. Deals with funds transfer pricing, issues of allocating and recovery and regulatory issues. Contains a glossary and a bibliography of books and periodical articles.

204. Compton, Eric N. *Principles of Banking*. 3d ed. Washington, DC: American Bankers Association, 1988. 403p.

An introductory text extensively revised since its first edition in 1979 to take account of the new developments, internally and externally, in the banking industry. Deals with the basic banking functions such as documents and language of banking, deposits and the relationship with depositors, paying tellers' duties, check processing and collection, bank bookkeeping, bank loans and investments, regulation and examination, personnel and security, trust department and other bank services. Each chapter ends with questions for discussion and suggested reading. Appended are a list of sources of information and a glossary.

205. Corns, Marshall C. *How To Audit a Bank.* 2d ed. rev. Boston: Bankers Publishing Co., 1966. 442p.

A manual for the use of the bank directors' examining committee, the bank's own auditors or the public accountants. Outlines the procedures to be followed in setting up internal controls and how to operate a comprehensive audit program. May be somewhat out of date, but the basic principles are still valid.

206. Cox, Edwin B., et al. *The Bank Director's Handbook.* 2d ed. Dover, MA: Auburn House, 1986. 294p.

Covers those areas of the banking function and services of most concern to the bank director, including the responsibilities and legal concerns of the board of directors. Treats asset/liability management, bank capital issues, measuring management and bank performance and strategic planning, human resources management, technology, and the banking environment of the future.

207. Crosse, Howard D., and Hempel, George H. *Management Policies for Commercial Banks.* 3d ed. Englewood Cliffs, NJ: Prentice-Hall, 1980. 356p.

Textbook for students, guide for bank directors and a manual for junior bank officers. Emphasizes policy formation and implementation. Discusses the banking environment in the 80s, especially the issues of branching and holding companies. Concerns those matters that affect management's decisions. Deals with the acquisition of bank funds, and other policy matters. Reviews past trends in banking. Projects the outlook for legislation and technology.

208. Davis, Steven I. *The Management Function in International Banking.* New York: Wiley, 1979. 166p.

Reviews the development of today's international markets and describes the role played by senior management of an international banking department. Author interviewed officials of forty commercial banks in the U.S., Europe and Asia to determine how issues are resolved concerning overall strategy, the establishment of an organizational structure and management of an overseas network. Includes bibliography.

209. Edmister, Robert O. *Financial Institutions: Markets and Management.* 2d ed. New York: McGraw-Hill, 1986. 521p.

An intermediate-level text aims to give students a practical foundation on the operation and business management of financial institutions. Reviews the workings of the financial markets. Describes the business conducted by different financial institutions and the managerial methods applicable to most types. Relates public policy concerns to the operations of financial institutions. The appendixes include compound interest equivalents and interest rate tables. Selected references at the end of each chapter.

210. Frankston, Fred M.; Mecimore, Charles D.; and Cornick, Michael F. *Bank Accounting.* Washing-

ton, DC: American Bankers Association, 1984. 319p.

Official text for American Institute of Bankers course, and serves as a basic reference for bankers. Describes all accounting functions and their applications to the various departments and services of a bank. Includes a glossary and list of additional resources.

211. Friedman, David H. *Deposit Operations*. 2d ed. Washington, DC: American Bankers Association, 1987. 354p.

Designed for bankers new to the profession and for those who want current information. Examines the U.S. payments mechanism and check collection process, and the cost, regulatory issues and risks in the electronic funds transfer system. Describes the changes in the sources and use of funds, bank deposit management and strategies for marketing. Deals with ways banks create deposits and the range of cash management services. Points out the changes that may occur in the future and what banks must do to increase production and stay competitive.

212. Garcia, Ferdinand L. *How To Analyze a Bank Statement*. 7th ed. Boston: Bankers Publishing Co., 1985. 234p.

Standard guide for bank controllers and analysts, managers and directors, and others especially concerned with bank holding company operation. Designed to provide the tools needed for a review of analytical ratios and techniques to use in analyzing bank holding company statements. Emphasizes the SEC newly revised reporting requirements and the Federal Reserve System basic reporting form as of 1983. Regulatory changes of 1984 are not included, and references to current sources must be used to supplement this useful tool. Includes a bibliography and notes.

213. Giroux, Gary A., and Rose, Peter S. *Financial Forecasting in Banking: Methods and Applications.* Research for Business Decisions no. 37. Ann Arbor, MI: UMI Research Press, 1981. 188p.

    The result of a survey to determine what forecasting techniques are currently used by commercial banks, for what functions they are used, what major sources of forecast information are used, and whether bank forecasts are used in other optimization or simulation models. The authors' thesis is that the present competitive and risky banking environment makes effective forecasting imperative in order to avoid costly management errors and misjudgments. The last chapter reviews bank forecasting literature.

214. Gup, Benton E.; Fraser, Donald R.; and Kolari, James W. *Commercial Bank Management.* New York: Wiley, 1989. 521p.

    Text for those who want to learn about managing banks and their investments from a practical point of view. Gives an overview of the banking system and bank investments. Discusses bank assets, liabilities and equity. Emphasizes the lending activities, such as commercial lending principles and process, real estate lending and consumer lending. Describes asset/liability management, international banking and off-balance sheet products and services. References at the end of each chapter.

215. Hale, Robert H. *Credit Analysis: A Complete Guide.* New York: Wiley, 1983. 302p.

A general guidebook for bankers and credit analysts applicable to credit management in any country. Describes credit analysis, how to examine the corporate structure and to evaluate industry and managment, cashflow analysis and term loans, and how to write a credit analysis. Illustrated by eighteen credit problems and case studies. Also supported by a glossary of financial terms.

216. Harrington, R. *Asset and Liability Management by Banks.* Paris: Organization for Economic Cooperation and Development, 1987. 176p.

Another in the series of trends in banking structure and regulation in OECD countries. Describes the development of asset and liability management in the past and how it is practiced currently. Discusses the whole range of asset and liability management: short and long term, wholesale and retail deposits, international syndicated lending and small retail loans, and balance sheet and off-balance sheet items. Includes bibliography.

217. Haslem, John. *Commercial Bank Management.* Reston, VA: Reston Publishing Co., 1985. 482p.

A compilation of articles relevant to management of commercial banks. Includes discussion of the recent legislation, liquidity management, management of selected funds sources and management of selected assets. Describes electronic funds transfer, financial futures, and interstate banking.

218. Hempel, George H. *Funds Management under Deregulation: Selected Readings.* Washington, DC: American Bankers Association, 1981. 752p.

A book of readings dealing with the challenging environment in which bank fund decisions will be made in the 1980s; and illustrating how to measure banking returns and the trade-offs between the returns on and the risk of bank funds. Also discusses attracting and pricing of needed raw materials, managing a bank's money and liquidity position, lending, managing the investment portfolio, financing a bank's capital needs, interest sensitivity analysis, budgeting techniques and asset/liability management. Each section has a bibliography. There is also a general bibliography.

219. Hudson, Nigel R. L. *Money and Exchange Dealing in International Banking.* New York: Wiley, 1979. 135p.

Describes the history and theory of dealing in foreign exchange and deposits. From a management point of view explains the operation and organization of a dealing department, and the practice of the dealing function. Includes a short bibliography and glossary.

220. Jessup, Paul F. *Modern Bank Management.* St. Paul, MN: West, 1980. 591p.

Gives the new general manager or the specialist in one part of banking a comprehensive view of bank management in a context of change. Discusses management of bank deposits, cash items, investment loans, and the relation between bank capital decisions and current and future composition of a bank's portfolio. Describes strategies by which banking organizations expand into new domestic and international markets.

221. Johnson, Frank P., and Johnson, Richard D. *Commercial Bank Management.* Washington, DC: American Bankers Association, 1986. 694p.

A practical introduction to the management of day-to-day bank activities. Uses flowcharts and case studies to illustrate management strategies. Emphasizes profit maximization. The appendixes give sample accounting entries, additional reference material and a glossary.

222. Jones, David M. *Fed Watching and Interest Rate Projections: A Practical Guide.* 2d ed. New York: New York Institute of Finance, 1989. 225p.

Mr. Jones, a Fed watcher with Aubrey G. Lanston and Co., gives some practical advice to would-be watchers, those who analyze the markets and manage investment portfolios. Explains the work of the Federal Open Market Committee and the operation of the discount window. Describes how the Fed makes its decisions regarding monetary policy and interest rates, the influence of personal and economic factors, and the meaning of monetary targets. Discusses how monetary policy is implemented. Gives four rules for Fed watching. Shows what facts indicate Federal Reserve policy shifts. The appendixes include excerpts from FOMC minutes, statistical tables, and release dates for Fed statistics.

223. Kammert, James L. *International Commercial Banking Management..* New York: AMACOM, 1981. 403p.

     Designed for members of various international units of banks, boards of directors and senior management. Describes the organization of international banking and its services, and explains the planning, people, procedures and problems involved. Appendixes include illustrations of procedures and forms, a listing of international banking schools, conferences and training programs, a checklist of factors used in country analysis, and other items.

224. Koch, Timothy W. *Bank Management.* Chicago: Dryden Press, 1988. 717p.

     Uses traditional concepts of business finance, and applies them to management of commercial banks. Each section introduces a problem, discusses the relevant financial concepts within an analytical framework, and shows, by sample data, the application of the relevant decision tools. Gives an overview of commercial bank management, and discusses asset and liability management strategies, planning models for estimating and meeting legal reserve requirements, the role of investment securities and financial futures, credit analysis, and international and trust banking.

225. Kolari, James W., and Zardkooki, Asghar. *Bank Cost, Structure, and Performance.* Lexington, MA: Lexington, 1987. 240p.

     Designed to give bank managers an understanding of how new financial services, such as automatic tellers, credit cards, banking by telephone, and corporate cash-management systems affect the economics of banking. Shows the need for strict cost controls to meet increasing bank competition. Reviews the literature in the cost economy of banking. Discusses the recent empirical evidence in the competitive environment. Two tables show overviews of the Depository Institutions Deregulation and Monetary Control Act of 1980 and of the Garn-St Germain Act. Includes a bibliography and notes.

226. Krumme, Dwane. *Banking and the Plastic Card.* Washington, DC: American Bankers Association, 1987. 263p.

Introduces the student and the banker to various types of bank credit cards. Traces the development of the cards, the credit process, consumer relations, regulation and management process. Discusses some of the important issues facing the banking industry in the use of the cards. Includes glossary.

227. McKinley, John E., et al. *Analyzing Financial Statements.* 2d ed. Washington, DC: American Bankers Association, 1984. 290p.

Basic text on statement analysis. Illustrates the analysis of past performance; and deals with analytical techniques to predict future performance. Illustrated with case studies and examples. Includes glossary.

228. Miller, Richard B. *Super Banking: Innovative Management Strategies (That Work).* Homewood, IL: Dow Jones-Irwin, 1989. 207p.

Looks at several banks that are doing exceptionally well in order to show what can be done to turn a bank around and to deal with the challenge of mergers and acquisitions. Shows what effective controls are needed to manage credit risk, the use of technology and statewide decentralized operations. Examines the ways to develop business by taking advantage of community needs, maximizing the marketing effort and offering specialized services.

229. Nadler, Paul S., and Miller, Richard B. *The Banking Jungle: How To Survive and Prosper in a Business Turned Topsy Turvy.* New York: Wiley, 1985. 443p.

Designed to give bankers and thrift executives practical ideas of how to survive in the changing financial environment in which banks have moved into the realm of big business. Discusses the need for bankers to meet the demands of a more sophisticated public in the use of money and the need to innovate in order to attract competent employees to deal with the changes brought about by computers. Deals with problems related to mergers and acquisitions, marketing and competition. Describes the function and responsibilities of bank directors.

230. Nagan, Peter S. *The Fed-Watchers Handbook: Everything You always Wanted To Know about Federal Reserve Policy Making.* Washington, DC: Goldsmith-Nagan, Inc., 1988. 82p.

Written in collaboration with the editors of the *ROG/Bond and Money Market Letter,* designed to dispel many of the myths and misunderstandings about the Fed's operations in and influence on the financial markets. A down-to-earth description of the process by which those who make monetary policy arrive at their decisions. Includes profiles of the policy makers and describes a typical policy shift.

231. Patten, James A. *Fundamentals of Bank Accounting.* Reston, VA: Reston Publishing Co., 1983. 285p.

    Basic text for college students and teachers and a handbook for bankers. Describes in detail each major balance sheet category, and analyzes the topics of the profit and statement. Includes bibliography.

232. Pezzullo, Mary Ann. *Marketing for Bankers.* 3d ed. Washington, DC: American Bankers Association, 1988. 564p.

    Advanced text and handbook illustrates marketing techniques that can be used in selling banking services. Emphasizes the personal approach necessary for successful marketing.

233. Pierce, James L., and Chase, Samuel B. *The Management of Risk in Banking.* Washington, DC: Association of Reserve City Bankers, 1988. 70p.

    A primer on risks faced by banks prepared for the Association of Reserve City Bankers. Explains the management of major types of risks such as credit, interest rate, off-balance sheet risks. Describes the role of government regulation and supervision and part played by liquidity, capital, asset and loan management policies in risk management.

234. Prochnow, Herbert V., ed. *Bank Credit.* New York: Harper & Row, 1981. 427p.

    Comprehensive description and analysis of the operation of a bank credit department. Written by practitioners, bankers and lawyers who consider all factors that enter into the granting of credit and various types of loans. Illustrated from everyday experiences of small

and large banks in various parts of the United
States.

235. Reed, Edward W., and Gill, Edward K. *Commercial Banking*. 4th ed. Englewood Cliffs, NJ:
Prentice-Hall, 1989. 472p.

A review of the management of commercial
banks that gives the professional and student an
analysis of the operation of a bank's many
functions. Describes the new environment in
which bank managers must operate. Deals with
the structure, organization and management of
banks; the management of deposits, cash and
liquidity items; lending, investing and trust
services; international banking, capital structure
and profitability. Each topic is considered in
relation to banking laws and regulations.

236. Richardson, Linda. *Banking in the Selling Role: A
Consultative Guide To Cross Selling*. 2d ed. New
York: Wiley, 1984. 177p.

The concepts of the book were shaped in
consultation with one thousand bankers. Discusses the present day competition for financial
services among banks and nonbank financial
houses that compels the banker to sell the bank's
services. Shows how a sales strategy can be
developed for a client's needs. Includes sales tips
and a checklist designed as a self-training device.

237. Rose, Peter S., and Fraser, Donald R. *Financial
Institutions; Understanding and Managing Financial Services*. 3d ed. Plano, TX: Business Publications, 1988. 762p.

Deals with key problem areas in the management of banks and other financial institutions,
including thrifts and contractual financial insti-

tutions. Includes areas of financial decision making that have become increasingly important, such as asset/liability management, hedging techniques, and selling and managing new sources of funds.

238. Roussakis, Emmanuel N. *Commercial Banking in an Era of Deregulation.* 2d ed. New York: Praeger, 1989. 428p.

Concerned with describing for the professional and the student the problems for management posed by deregulation, electronic data processing and telecommunications and increased competition. Gives an overview of the U.S. commercial banking system and its environment. Treats the sources of bank funds and the policy objectives in the employment of bank funds. Describes the uses of bank funds and the characteristics of bank assets. Emphasizes the deregulation movement which is leading to growing competition and overlap of functions between banks and other depository institutions. There are bibliographic notes at the end of each chapter.

239. Savage, John H. *Bank Audits and Examinations: A Detailed Step-by-Step Program for CPA's, Bank Internal Auditors, Bank Directors, and Bank Examiners.* 2d ed. Boston: Bankers Publishing Co., 1980. 194p.

A guide, in working paper form, illustrating practical procedures for the examination of any bank department.

240. Shout, Esther M. *Internal Bank Auditing.* New York: Wiley, 1982. 249p.

Aimed at bank employees and officers, and

others not directly concerned with auditing, but who should be familiar with the theory, techniques, objectives and standards of internal auditing. Appendixes include applicable banking laws and regulations, and the Comptroller of the Currency's Handbook for National Bank Examiners. There is a bibliography.

241. Stigum, Marcia L., and Branch, Rene O., Jr. *Managing Bank Assets & Liabilities; Strategies for Risk Control & Profit*. Homewood, IL: Dow Jones-Irwin, 1983. 429p.

A guide for bankers on how to manage a bank's assets and liabilities so as to maximize profits. Useful to bankers, either commercial or thrift, large or small; and of interest to dealers, analysts and others concerned with banks' financial situations. Provides a background for those new in the field and an overview of the money market. Treats in detail the tactics and strategies for managing liquidity, and forecasting interest rates. There is a chapter on futures with an appendix that details the various kinds of financial futures and hedging; a chapter on foreign currency dealings; and a postscript on the "banking debacles" occurring as the book went to press. A glossary and index add to the book's usefulness.

242. U.S. Comptroller General. *Bank Failures; Independent Audits Needed To Strengthen Internal Control and Bank Management*. Washington, DC: General Accounting Office, 1989. 86p.

A review of the documents related to the 184 insured banks that failed in 1987. Study found that weak internal controls contributed to the failures, but that insider abuse and fraud were not major factors. Points out that proper internal controls serve as a buffer against adverse outside conditions and that independent audits detect internal control weaknesses.

243. Wittkowske, Fred; Polaris, Mark F.; and Coen, Charles D. *Internal Auditing in the Banking Industry.* Park Ridge, IL: Bank Administration Institute, 1984. 3 vols.

Purpose is to give complete coverage of the field with emphasis on professionalism; and to provide materials that will be useful to practitioners and to students as a text or supplemental reading. Volume I reviews the general audit principles and methods; Volume II discusses the auditing of the basic bank functions relating to assets; and Volume III concerns the auditing of basic bank functions relating to liabilities.

9. BANK AUTOMATION

244. Bender, Mark G. *EFTS Electronic Funds Transfer Systems; Elements and Impact.* Port Washington, NY: Kennikat, 1975. 99p.

    For those who wish a quick overview of the early developments of the automated exchange mechanism, this text will introduce the nonexpert to the major forces that have precipitated the transition to an electronic payments mechanism, the major elements of that mechanism, some attendant issues involved and the probable economic implications. Of special interest is the list of unresolved issues, some of which remain unresolved today.

245. Colton, Kent W., and Kraemer, Kenneth L., eds. *Computers and Banking: Electronic Funds Transfer Systems and Public Policy.* New York: Plenum, 1980. 309p.

    Based, in part, on papers presented at the Conference on EFT Research and Public Policy held in 1977 in Boston. Includes articles on the state and outlook for EFT technology and an assessment of EFT services in the United States, the present and potential impact of EFT on society, the economy, and on regulation and control. Includes an agenda for EFT research. Can be read as a companion to Bender.

246. Jackson, D. Mark. *1986 Survey of the Electronic Funds Transfer System.* Rolling Meadows, IL: Bank Administration Institute, 1987. 150p.

Survey among commercial banks of their experience with electronic funds transfer transactions. Gives results of ACHs (automated clearing houses), ATMs (automated teller machines) and POSs (point-of-sales).

247. Lam, Chun H., and Hempel, George H. *Microcomputer Applications in Banking*. New York: Quorum Books, 1986. 206p.

Traces the history and development of computing machinery, and how the microcomputer system works. Illustrates, using case studies, the application of microcomputers to various bank management areas. Speculates about future applications of microcomputers to management and communications. Appendix shows the use of microcomputer applications using Lotus 1-2-3. Includes bibliography.

248. Lipis, Allen H.; Marshall, Thomas R.; and Linker, Jan H. *Electronic Banking*. New York: Wiley, 1985. 220p.

Based on over 200 studies conducted by the authors for Electronic Banking, Inc., the book is designed to further a better understanding by the financial industry of electronic banking within the present environment. Focuses on retail services, wholesale aspects and the future of electronic banking services.

249. National Commission on Electronic Fund Transfers. *EFT in the United States; Policy Recommendation and the Public Interest*. Washington, DC: Government Printing Office, 1977. 149p.

The final report of a commission established by Congress and appointed by the President to conduct a thorough study and investigation of

the emerging payments system and to recom-
mend appropriate administrative action and
legislation to permit the orderly development of
private and public EFT systems. A good picture
of the state of EFT at that time.

250. Revell, J. R. S. *Banking and Electronic Fund
Transfers.* Paris: Organization for Economic
Cooperation and Development, 1983. 190p.

Part of study on trends in banking structure
and regulation in OECD countries. An economic analysis of the implications for banking in
OECD member countries of technological
changes. Discusses the whole range of automation within banks and between banks. Goes
beyond the payments system to describe other
electronic techniques such as dealing networks
for money market instruments, securities and
foreign currencies, registration systems for securities and various information systems. Shows
how the changes have affected the business of
banking and its regulation. There is a list of
references.

10. STATISTICS

251. American Bankers Association. *Statistical Information on the Financial Services Industry.* 5th ed. Washington, DC, 1989. 300p.

   Describes the market for financial services with emphasis on commercial banks and other depository institutions. Gives a wide variety of data for the years 1975–1985, including profitability, capital, structure, sources and use of funds. Discusses the payments system, consumer attitudes and trends, and trends in financial assets and liabilities in nonfinancial sectors. Includes demographic and other market data.

252. Board of Governors of the Federal Reserve System. *All-Bank Statistics; United States, 1896–1955.* Washington, DC, 1959. 1229p.

   A consistent series of statistics for commercial and mutual savings banks by class of bank and by state.

253. Board of Governors of the Federal Reserve System. *Banking and Monetary Statistics.* Washington, DC, 1943. 979p.

   A comprehensive compilation of statistics relating mainly to commercial banking and related financial markets, 1914–1941. Data originally published in the *Federal Reserve Bulletin* and in the annual reports before 1938.

254. Board of Governors of the Federal Reserve System. *Banking and Monetary Statistics, 1941–1970.* Washington, DC, 1976. 1229p.

Brings the earlier volume up-to-date, although it does not include all the series. Kept current by *Annual Statistical Digest.*

11. BIBLIOGRAPHIES, DICTIONARIES, AND ENCYCLOPEDIAS

255. Balachandran, M. *A Guide to Statistical Sources in Money, Banking & Finance.* Phoenix, AZ: Oryx Press, 1988. 119p.

     Lists sources of statistics for states, regions, U.S., foreign countries, and international. Includes databases and a directory of publishers, as well as title and subject indexes.

256. *Banking Terminology.* 3d ed. Washington, DC: American Bankers Association, 1989. 409p.

     Designed to assist managers in managing daily business activities. Includes 5,000 entries of terms and phrases used in all areas of banking. Practical for desk use.

257. *Business and Economics Books, 1876–1983.* New York: R. R. Bowker Co., 1983. 4 vols.

     A comprehensive documentation of over 100 years of business and economics books in the United States. The first three volumes are trade books by subject. The fourth volume is the author index.

258. Jud, G. Donald, and Woelfel, Charles J. *The Desktop Encyclopedia of Banking.* Chicago: Probus, 1988. 397p.

Brief descriptions of more than 300 concepts, terms, issues, and procedures needed by bankers and others involved in banking and finance. Contains references to current literature. Illustrated by charts and graphs.

259. Monk, J. Thomas; Landis, Kenneth M.; and Monk, Susan S. *The Dow Jones-Irwin Banker's Guide to Online Databases.* Homewood, IL: Richard D. Irwin, 1988. 587p.

Discusses the pros and cons of online information. Describes the industry and the criteria by which to choose the databases needed. Lists more than 190 leading online products and their vendors. Explains what enabling telecommunications and software are needed to use and to enhance the use of the databases. Appendixes give lists of providers and gateways.

260. Munn, Glenn G., and Garcia, Ferdinand L. *Encyclopedia of Banking and Finance.* 8th rev. ed. Boston: Bankers Publishing Co., 1983. 1024p.

The standard reference book, answers most questions on the history and structure of banking, defines terms, and describes major laws and legislation pertaining to American banking, including the Depository Institutions Deregulation and Monetary Control Act of 1980 and the Garn-St Germain Act of 1982. There are short bibliographies at the end of each major section.

261. *Online Databases in the Securities and Financial Markets.* New York: Cuadra/Elsevier, 1987. 322p.

Thirteen hundred entries list 1655 databases for 33 industries. The introductory material gives an overview of online database services, and how to select and use databases. The directory lists addresses of online services and gateways. Includes subject, online service/gateway, and master indexes.

262. Rachlin, Harvey, ed. *The Money Encyclopedia.* New York: Harper & Row, 1984. 669p.
    Short articles contributed by people in government, stock and commodity exchanges, trade and professional associations, academic institutions and others. The major entries are current through the end of 1983 and include insurance, accounting, mortgages, money market, banking and other financial institutions.

263. Ricci, Julio, comp. *Elsevier's Banking Dictionary in Six Languages: English/American, French, Italian, Spanish, Dutch and German.* 2d rev. ed. Amsterdam: Elsevier, 1980. 286p.
    English terms are arranged alphabetically with terms in other languages listed beneath. In a separate section the non-English terms are listed in one alphabet with page references to the English section.

264. Rosenberg, Jerry M. *Dictionary of Banking and Financial Services.* 2d ed. New York: Wiley, 1985. 708p.
    Includes approximately 15,000 entries and incorporates the 1981 edition of the ABA's *Banking Terminology.* Includes recent banking legislation. Supplement contains statistical information on the banking and financial institutions, as well as information on banking hours for countries and states, holidays, state banking authorities and associations, and computational tables.

265. Seglin, Jeffrey L. *Bank Administration Manual; A Comprehensive Reference Guide.* 3d ed. rev. Rolling Meadows, IL: Bank Administration Institute, 1988. 427p.

A ready reference to major terms and concepts of banking. Entries are arranged alphabetically by title with a short description or definition. Articles are cross-referenced and related entries are cited. There are suggested readings at the end of most articles. Table of contents arranged as an index.

266. U.S. Congress. House. Committee on Banking, Finance and Urban Affairs. *List of Publications.* Washington, DC: Government Printing Office, 1982. 192p.

Indexed alphabetically by title and by Congress, includes hearings, reports and committee prints issued from 1864 to 1980. This and the following congressional listings are handy references to legislative activities related to banking.

267. U.S. Congress. Senate. Committee on Banking and Currency. *Publications of the Senate Banking and Currency Committee, together with the Joint Committee on Defense Production, 81st and 82d Congress.* Washington, DC: Government Printing Office, 1952. 20p.

Hearings, reports, public laws, special laws by subject under Congress for the period 1949–1952.

268. U.S. Congress. Senate. Committee on Banking and Currency. *Publications of the Committee on Banking and Currency, 83d-85th Congress.* Wash-

ington, DC: Government Printing Office, 1959. 27p.
Covers 1953–1958.

269. U.S. Congress. Senate. Committee on Government Operations. *Select List of Publications . . . Issued by Senate and House Committees.* Washington, DC: Government Printing Office, 1961. 427p.
Lists committee prints, staff studies, reports and documents from 1947 to 1960. Does not include House Banking and Currency Committee legislation and reports.

12. SERIALS

A. Indexes

270. *ABI/INFORM*. Louisville, KY: UMI/Data Courier. Updated weekly.

Electronic database giving summaries of more than 400,000 articles covering a wide field of interest to business including banking and finance. Full text of articles are available through UMI/Data Courier. Available through a number of timesharing systems, including DIALOG and Mead Data Central.

271. *American Statistics Index*. Washington, DC: Congressional Information Service, 1974—. Monthly with Annual.

Volume 1 abstracts statistical data published by major governmental statistical and research agencies, as well as regulatory agencies, congressional committees, judicial offices, special councils, commissions and boards. Includes periodicals, series, special reports, annuals and biennials. Volume 2 indexes publications by subject, name, type of data breakdown, publication and agency report number with reference number to abstract volume which gives full description of the data. Available online.

272. *Banking Literature Index*. Washington, DC: American Bankers Association, 1982—. Monthly with annual cumulation.

Subject index to current periodical articles on banking trends, topics, issues and operations. Focuses on practical banking management. Does not include editorials, news stories, book reviews or conference articles.

273. *Bibliographic Guide to Business and Economics.* Boston: G. K. Hall, 1975—. 3 vols. Annual.

Subject bibliographies bring together the publications cataloged by the Research Libraries of the New York Public Library and by the Library of Congress. Source for all major publications including books, serials and non-book publications in banking and related fields.

274. *Business and Economics Books and Serials in Print.* New York: R. R. Bowker, 1977–1981. Annual.

A companion to the four-volume index *Business and Economics Books, 1876–1983,* lists 37,500 titles by author, title and subject. The 1981 volume lists over 6,000 serials. No longer published, but still a useful tool for retrospective searches.

275. *Business Periodicals Index.* New York: Wilson, 1958—. Monthly, except August, with periodic cumulations.

Index to over 300 English language periodicals by subject in all fields of business including banking. Prior to 1957 included in the *Industrial Arts Index.* Available online.

276. *CIS/Index.* Washington, DC: Congressional Information Service, 1970—. Monthly with Annual.

Published in two volumes. In index volume, publications are arranged by subject, name, title,

author, bill number and publication number
giving reference to the abstract volume. Abstract volume analyzes in detail over 300 publications of the House and Senate. The indexes
and abstracts are cumulated in an annual
volume which also includes legislative history
and citations to public laws enacted during the
year. Available online.

277. *Fed in Print*. Philadelphia, PA: Federal Reserve
Bank of Philadelphia, 1973—. Two times per
year.
   Includes all publications of the Federal Reserve Board's and the twelve Federal Reserve
Banks' research departments beginning with
1969.

278. *FINIS: Financial Industry Information Service*.
Chicago: Bank Marketing Association, 1982—.
   An online database containing marketing information for the financial services industry.
Includes abstracts from about 200 journals,
books, press releases, sample brochures and
reports. Also includes abstracts of outstanding
student projects from BMA schools, and records
of the BMA "Golden Coin" Award entries.
Accessed through DIALOG, NEXIS, and others.

279. *Index of Economic Articles*. Homewood, IL: Irwin,
1961—. Annual.
   Prepared under the auspices of the American
Economic Association. Indexes by author and
subject, articles in major economic journals
and in collections. Volumes are an adjunct
to the *Journal of Economic Literature*. Available
online.

280. *Index to the American Banker.* Wooster, OH: Bell & Howell, 1971—. Monthly with quarterly and annual cumulations.

Indexes articles appearing in the leading daily newspaper for bankers. Divided into three sections: General subjects, personal names and corporations.

281. *Journal of Economic Literature.* Nashville, TN: American Economic Association, 1963—. Quarterly.

Contains abstracts and bibliographic citations from nearly 300 journals, also book reviews on a broad subject range within the field of economics. A companion to *Index to Economic Articles.* Available online.

282. *Monthly Catalog of United States Government Publications.* Washington, DC: Government Printing Office, 1951—. Monthly with semiannual and annual indexes.

Comprehensive catalog of U.S. government agency, departmental and congressional publications. Gives full bibliographic entry with subject headings. Listed by author or issuing agent. Indexes include title, subject, series/report, contract number, stock number, and title keyword. Periodicals are listed in a separate supplement.

283. National Technical Information Service. *Business & Economics; An Abstract Newsletter.* Springfield, VA, 1977—. Weekly.

One of a series of abstract bulletins published by the National Technical Information Service of the Department of Commerce. Contains abstracts of recent U.S. and foreign government research reports. Available online.

284. *PAIS Bulletin.* New York: Public Affairs Information Service, 1915—. Semimonthly with three cumulations and annual.

Selective list of latest books, pamphlets, government publications, reports of public and private agencies and periodical articles relating to business, including banking, and related fields published in English throughout the world. Available online.

285. *Statistical Reference Index.* Washington, DC: Congressional Information Service, 1980—. Monthly with annual cumulation.

Volume 1 abstracts statistical publications of 1,000 associations and institutes, business and research organizations, commercial publishers, state agencies and universities. Volume 2 contains indexes by subjects, names, categories, issuing sources and titles with references to the abstract volume which describes the publications in detail. A good source for data published by states and municipalities.

286. *World Banking Abstracts; comp. by Institute of European Finance, University College of North Wales.* Rolling Meadows, IL: Bank Administration Institute. Bi-Monthly.

Abstracts articles from over 400 periodicals, research reports and studies worldwide. Designed for the decision maker in financial institutions, subjects include international conditions, banking business, banking and other institutions, securities and markets, policy and regulation, management and accounting, and general information.

B. Directories, Yearbooks, and Annual Reports

287. American Banker. *Top Numbers*. New York, 1987—. Annual.

     Originally entitled *American Banker Yearbook*. A reference book for financial services executives. Contains the latest banking industry statistics, articles on key trends and developments, important dates for the year and projected dates of influence for the year ahead, listings of key addresses, and of largest financial institutions.

288. *American Bank Directory*. Norcross, GA: McFadden Business Publications, 1836—. Semiannual.

     Alphabetical list of all banks in the United States, including national, state, savings and private banks. Arranged by state, shows names of officers, directors and principal correspondents plus a statement of condition. Useful desk reference.

289. *American Savings Directory*. Norcross, GA: McFadden Business Publications, 1981—. Annual.

     Desk handbook lists savings and loans, major credit unions, all mutual savings banks and all money market funds. Arranged alphabetically by state and city and includes financial data.

290. *Annual Review of Banking Law*. Boston: Morin Center for Banking Law Studies, Boston University, 1982—.

Initial article reviews developments in banking law for the past year. This is followed by contributed essays on the legal and regulatory aspects of leading issues in banking.

291. Association of Bank Holding Companies. *Bank Holding Company Facts*. Washington, DC, 1958—. Semiannual.

Lists offices and deposits of banks affiliated with bank holding companies by years, banks, offices, deposits and assets of association member companies, largest bank affiliated with each association member company, officers and directors of the Association of Bank Holding Companies, chief elected officers of the association, charter members and the annual meetings of the association.

292. *The Bankers' Almanac and Yearbook*. East Grinstead, England: Thomas Skinner Directories, 1845—. Semiannual.

Popularly known as "Skinner's," this is the standard reference on international banks of the world. Volume 1 contains the listing of over 3,600 major banks in one alphabetical sequence plus a geographical index. Listings include the address, telephone and other communications numbers, date established, top officers, correspondents, consolidated balance sheet, dividends, meetings, branches, subsidiaries and associated companies. Volume 2 contains an alphabetical list of countries. Under each country there is a list of towns and within each town a list of the banks that have a branch, agency or representative office. In addition there is much miscellaneous information and statistics mostly of British interest.

293. *Bankers Schools Directory.* Washington, DC: American Bankers Association, 1978—. Biannual.

A list of banking schools sponsored by the American Bankers Association, state bankers associations, and other national and regional groups offering courses, seminars and workshops designed for those interested in banking, finance, economics and management, particularly for those working in the field. Alphabetical by name of school. Includes state and subject indexes. The appendix contains a brief explanation of ABA's American Institute of Banking which administers local and self-study educational programs; and a description of ABA's Professional Development Program in Banking.

294. *The Banks in Your State.* Austin, TX: Sheshunoff, 1975—. Volume for each state. Semiannual.

Comprehensive overview of banks within the state, in-depth analysis of balance sheet and income statements, including deposits, loans, income, and capital adequacy, with projections. Sheshunoff also publishes similar volumes for bank holding companies, mutual savings banks and savings and loan associations.

295. Board of Governors of the Federal Reserve System. *Annual Statistical Digest.* Washington, DC, 1980—. Annual.

Brings up-to-date much of the data in *Banking and Monetary Statistics* and maintains a historical series for tables published in the *Federal Reserve Bulletin*. Data are given for five year periods.

296. Board of Governors of the Federal Reserve System. *Historical Chart Book*. Washington, DC. Annual.

 Over one hundred charts that show long-range financial and business trends from 1800.

297. *Callahan's Credit Union Directory*. Washington, DC: Callahan & Associates, 1986—. Annual.

 Financial data include rankings of credit unions by fastest growing, largest by assets, by members, by reserves, and by capital ratios. Credit unions are listed alphabetically by state and show name, address, CEO, assets, loans, investments, capital, members, percentage of growth.

298. Cox, Edwin B. *Bank Performance Annual*. Boston: Warren, Gorham & Lamont, 1987—. Annual.

 Designed to provide bank managers with up-to-date information that will guide them to improve the financial and operating perform-ance of their banks. Reviews the developments of the past year that will affect the events of the coming year. Contains articles by experts giving advice on areas of management responsibility. Profiles major segments of the financial indus-try with statistics. Includes a directory of promi-nent financial industry associations and regula-tory agencies.

299. Decision Research Sciences, Inc. *Branch Directory and Summary of Deposits with Market Indicators*. Blue Bell, PA, 1975—. 16 vols. Annual.

County summary shows five categories of deposits for commercial banks, mutual savings banks, savings and loans, federal savings banks and credit unions. Geographic section lists all commercial and mutual savings banks, S&Ls, federal savings banks, cooperative banks and credit unions by county and by city within county, and financial institutions within cities. Includes a Zip-code summary section, a financial institutions section, and a bank holding company section.

300. *Directory of American Savings and Loan Associations.* Baltimore, MD: T. K. Sanderson Organization, 1955—. Annual.

Aims at a complete listing of all active savings and/or building and loan associations, cooperative banks and savings banks by states.

301. *Euromoney International Finance Yearbook.* London: Euromoney Publications, 1987—. Annual.

Part I contains short articles about the current state of their business by senior bankers from principal banking centers throughout the world. Part II contains reviews written by leading practitioners of all important financial products and markets such as debt management, equity financing, new technology, international trade and commodity markets. Part III is a databank of statistics covering foreign exchange rates, interest rates, financial futures rates, currency-adjusted equity, bank and money market returns. Includes annual as well as historical tables.

302. Federal Deposit Insurance Corporation. *Annual Report.* Washington, DC, 1934—. Annual.

Covers FDIC operations. Summarizes bank supervision, deposit protection, enforcement activities, and new regulations and legislation. Statistical section shows number and deposits of banks closed and insured banks requiring disbursements by the FDIC.

303. Federal Deposit Insurance Corporation. *Data Book: Operating Banks and Branches . . . Summary of Deposits in All Commercial and Mutual Savings Banks.* Washington, DC, 1980—. 19 vols. Annual.

Data for all banks by insurance status and class of bank, for all insured commercial and insured and reporting noninsured mutual savings banks, by size of bank and by SMSA (Standard Metropolitan Statistical Area), by state for all insured and reporting noninsured banks, by insurance status and class of bank; and for state and county of all insured and reporting noninsured commercial and mutual savings banks. One volume for national data plus one volume for each district.

304. Federal Deposit Insurance Corporation. *Statistics on Banking.* Washington, DC, 1981—. Annual.

Statistics on FDIC insured commercial banks and trust companies. Tables cover number of banks and branches, bank finances in summary, assets and liabilities, income and expenses of savings banks, bank finances by state, and financial ratios.

305. Federal Financial Institutions Examination Council. *Annual Report.* Washington, DC, 1979—. Annual.

Report on the activities and finances of the FFIEC. Tables show financial statements for the Council and for commercial banks and thrifts.

306. Federal Financial Institutions Examination Council. *Trust Assets of Financial Institutions.* Washington, DC, 1979—. Annual.

Previously published jointly by the FDIC, Federal Reserve Board and the Comptroller of the Currency. Data, based on annual reports filed with the three regulatory agencies, show the trust assets and selected investment fund characteristics of commercial and savings banks, S&Ls and trust companies under their jurisdiction.

307. Federal Home Loan Bank Board. *Annual Report.* Washington, DC, 1933—. Annual.

Covers the activities and financial performance of the Federal Home Loan Bank Board, Federal Home Loan Banks, Federal Savings and Loan Insurance Corporation and Federal Home Loan Mortgage Corporation. Future publications of the Federal Home Loan Bank Board may be issued by the U.S. Office of Thrift Supervision, Savings Association Insurance Fund, Bank Insurance Fund, F.S.L.I.C. Resolution Fund, Federal Housing Finance Board or the Resolution Trust Corporation.

308. Federal Home Loan Bank Board. *Assets and Liability Trends; All Operating Saving and Loan Associations by Type of Association and by Area.* Washington, DC, 1948—. Annual.

Data for the past ten years are shown for selected years, and include trends from 1930 for insured and noninsured S&Ls.

309. Federal Home Loan Bank Board. *Combined Financial Statements, FSLIC Insured Institutions.* Washington, DC, 1946—. Annual.

    Financial data on savings institutions insured by FSLIC and summary data on federally chartered savings banks insured by FDIC.

310. Federal Home Loan Bank Board. *Members of the Federal Home Loan Bank System.* Washington, DC, 1966—. Annual.

    Listed by type of institution showing docket number, address, and, for insured institutions only, assets. Arranged by state, Guam, Puerto Rico, and by city. Appendix of listed savings and loan holding companies.

311. Federal Home Loan Bank Board. *Saving and Home Financing Source Book.* Washington, DC, 1955—. Annual.

    Report on FHLBB finances, savings institutions' lending activity and financial conditions, mortgage terms and debt outstanding of all types of lenders, with trends from 1900.

312. Federal Home Loan Bank Board. *Summary of Savings Accounts by Geographic Area: FSLIC Insured Institutions.* Washington, DC, 1967—. Annual.

    Presents dollar volume of accounts by offices and summary basis for areas. Data include numbers of FSLIC insured institutions and offices by size classes, and total savings accounts.

313. Federal Reserve Bank of Kansas City. *Banking Studies.* Kansas City, MO, 1983—. Annual.

    Report on banking industry structure, performance, and other characteristics in the Federal Reserve 10th district. Recent supplements concern problem banks and community banks.

314. Federal Reserve Bank of New York. *Annual Report.* New York, 1916—. Annual.
First report covered 1914/15. Reviews banking and credit developments and U.S. monetary relations abroad. Feature article focuses on a major issue affecting banking or monetary conditions at home or abroad. Contains operating and other statistics for the second district. Other Federal Reserve Banks have annual reports or operating statements.

315. *Financial Services Yearbook.* Berkeley, CA: University of California Press, 1988—. Annual.
Sponsored by the National Center on Financial Services. Seeks to publish the best student research papers on topics of timely interest to the industry. First issue contains articles on bank credit cards, deposit insurance, bank failures, acquisition of thrifts across state lines and regulatory problems.

316. *Moody's Bank & Finance Manual.* New York: Moody's Investors Services, 1900—. 3 vols. Annual with twice weekly news reports.
A comprehensive directory of all financial institutions. Volume one lists banks and trust companies, savings and loan associations, and federal credit agencies. Basic manual summarizes corporate history, structure of each institution and its subsidiaries. Lists the officers and directors, and describes the financial condition of each institution. The news reports list any changes in the corporate structure and financial

picture. Volume two includes insurance, finance, real estate and investment companies. Volume three lists unit investment trusts. Available online.

317. National Council of Savings Institutions. *Directory.* Washington, DC, 1924—. Annual.

Successor to National Association of Mutual Savings Banks. List of Council's savings bank and savings and loan association members by state. Includes state and regional member trade organizations and international affiliates. The listings include names of key executives, type of charter, insuring agency, form of ownership, balance sheet data, membership in Federal Home Loan Bank System, and a CEO locator index.

318. National Council of Savings Institutions. *Fact Book of Savings Institutions.* Washington, DC, 1984—. Annual.

Previously published by the National Association of Mutual Savings Banks. Highlights the year's developments in the savings industry. Gives national statistics on portfolio and deposit activity, mortgage and housing, income and investment. State statistics cover portfolio and deposit activity, and income and investment. Includes a glossary.

319. National Credit Union Administration. *Annual Report.* Washington, DC, 1943—. Annual.

Covers the operations of the NCUA and includes reports on the National Credit Union Share Insurance Fund and the National Credit Union Central Liquidity Facility.

320. National Credit Union Administration. *Directory of All Federally Insured Credit Unions.* Washington, DC, 1983—. Annual.

Arranged alphabetically by state, contains names of all federally chartered credit unions and state-chartered CUs insured by the National Credit Union Share Insurance Fund. Shows charter or state insurance credit number, name, address, name of principal operating officer, telephone number and assets.

321. National Credit Union Administration. *Year End Statistics.* Washington, DC, 1984—. Annual.

Includes Federal Credit Unions and federally insured state-chartered credit unions. Data cover assets, liabilities, earnings and expenses, operations and other information by region and state, and by type of membership. Also issues a midyear statistical report.

322. *Polk's Bank Directory.* Nashville, TN: Polk & Company, 1894—. Twice per year with bi-monthly supplements. International edition published annually at mid-year.

Lists all commercial and mutual savings banks in the United States by states and cities. Also lists some banks in Canada, Mexico, Central America and the Caribbean. Gives the officers and directors, correspondents, out-of-town branches and latest balance sheet information. Lists the regulatory agencies and trade associations, national and state. Includes maps, bank holding companies and transit numbers.

323. *Principles & Presentation: Banking; a Review of . . . Annual Reports.* New York: KPMG Peat Marwick, 1976—. Irregular.

Study of accounting principles and financial statements used by America's largest banks in their annual reports. Reviews latest developments affecting bank auditing. Comments on the statements are reproduced in the last chapter.

324. *Principles & Presentation: Thrifts; a Review of . . . Annual Reports.* New York: KPMG Peat Marwick, 1976—. Irregular.

Reviews the annual reports for thrifts in the same format as its coverage for banks.

325. *The Rand McNally Bankers Directory.* Chicago, 1876—. 3 vols. Semiannual.

First two volumes contain individual listing of every head office, branch, agency, representative office and banking Edge Act corporation located in the United States. Each listing has address and telephone number, balance sheet data and names of key administrative staff. The third volume contains individual listing of all offices of international banks involved in foreign exchange or foreign trade. Includes selected reference and statistical information on banks, regulatory agencies and bank holding companies.

326. *The Rand McNally Credit Union Directory.* Chicago, 1986—. Annual.

A handbook listing all credit unions; organized alphabetically by state and by city within each state. Gives the name, address, managing officer, charter number, year established, number of credit union members, routing number, and financial summary.

327. *Thorndike Encyclopedia of Banking and Financial Tables.* Boston: Warren, Gorham & Lamont, l980—. Annual.

   Handbook for bankers, especially loan and trust officers. Contains mortgage amortization schedules, banking and financial information with tables of interest rates and foreign exchange rates. Includes a section on laws concerning state interest rate ceilings, bad check laws, taxation, international weights and measures, glossaries and an index.

328. United States League of Savings Institutions. *Savings Institutions Sourcebook.* Chicago, 1984—. Annual.

   Data cover savings, mortgage lending, housing, savings institutions operations, and federal government agencies. Includes glossary.

329. *The U.S. Savings and Loan Directory.* Chicago: Rand McNally, 1982—. 2 vols. Annual.

   Comprehensive source of information on all savings and loans nationwide. Includes an alphabetical index of savings institutions, federal and state information, industry information, and routing numbers. State sections are preceded by map, demographic and statistical information, a list of financial institutions, S&Ls, banks and credit unions. The S&L listings include officers, routing numbers, correspondents, financial data and branches.

330. *Who's Who in International Banking.* London: International Insider, 1987—. Annual?

Contains listing of 4,000 senior bank officers working for major international banks. Lists each bank and its most senior international officer on a country by country basis, and major borrowers in the international markets and their senior treasury officials.

C. Periodicals and Newspapers

331. *ABA Bank Compliance.* Washington, DC: American Bankers Association, 1980—. Eight times per year.

     Quarterly issues contain articles on regulatory and legislative activity pertaining to banking. The four issues in between are newsletters that update that information. (BLI)

332. *ABA Banking Journal.* New York: Simmons Boardman, 1908—. Monthly.

     Official journal of the American Bankers Association. Articles cover latest developments in banking, information on products and services, and operating advice. (BPI, PAIS, BLI, online)

333. *American Banker.* New York: American Banker, Inc., 1836—. Daily.

     The major U.S. banking newspaper. Has its own index. (BLI, online)

334. *Bank Administration.* Rolling Meadows, IL: Bank Administration Institute, 1925—. Monthly.

     Articles on strategic planning, marketing, capital and financial planning, mergers and acquisitions, automation and technological developments, and other issues of concern to senior bank managers. (BLI, online)

335. *Bank Expansion Quarterly.* Washington, DC: Golembe Associates, 1972—. Quarterly.
Financial data on mergers and acquisitions among financial institutions.

336. *Bank Letter.* New York: Institutional Investor, 1977—. Weekly.
News and commentary on the banking industry.

337. *Bank Marketing.* Chicago: Bank Marketing Association, 1969—. Monthly.
Covers developments in all areas of financial services marketing, bank advertising, electronic banking, and public relations. (BPI, BLI, online)

338. *Bank Mergers & Acquisitions.* New York: Curran & Roemer, Inc., 1986—. Monthly.
Newsletter analyzing the latest merger and acquisitions developments.

339. *The Banker.* London: Financial Times Business Information, 1926—. Monthly.
Leading British banking periodical with world-wide coverage of banking developments as well as articles on bank operation and management. (BIS, BLI, PAIS, online)

340. *Banker International.* London: Euromoney Publications, 1987—. Monthly.
Articles of current interest plus regular sections on credit, news, results and accounts, mergers and acquisitions, openings and closings, and changes in official staffs.

341. *The Bankers Magazine.* Boston: Warren, Gorham & Lamont, 1886—. Six times per year.

     Articles of general interest in the field of banking. Washington report, short features on latest developments, and book reviews. (BPI, PAIS, BLI, online)

342. *Banker's Monthly.* New York: Hanover Publications, 1883—. Monthly.

     Articles, special features. Regular departments include inside banking, bond bulletin, marketing, bank capital markets, bank stock summary, and bankers bookshelf. (BPI, PAIS, BLI, online)

343. *Banking Expansion Reporter.* New York: Prentice Hall Law & Business, 1982—. Semi-monthly.

     Edited by Golembe Associates. Editorial comment on latest banking developments. Regular features include product expansion, geographic expansion and a section on regulatory and judicial matters, speeches, articles and documents. (BLI)

344. *Banking Law Journal.* Boston: Warren, Gorham & Lamont, 1889—. Six issues per year.

     Scholarly articles on legal developments in banking. Regular features include counsel's comments, banking briefs, banking decisions, books for bankers. (PAIS, BLI and online)

345. *Banking Week.* New York: American Banker, 1986—. Weekly.

     Designed for those who need to keep up with developments in the financial services industry, but do not need the detail of a newspaper such as the *American Banker.* Covers bank performance trends, federal and state regulation, marketing, technology, competition, mergers. Includes statistics and feature articles.

346. Board of Governors of the Federal Reserve System. *Statistical Releases.* Washington, DC. Weekly, Monthly, Quarterly.

Time series data on various financial, market and related economic topics. Data in some releases are reissued in *Federal Reserve Bulletin.* A complete schedule of releases is published in the June and December issues of the *Bulletin.* Available online.

347. *Bottomline.* Washington, DC: National Council of Savings Institutions, 1983—. Monthly.

Merger of *Savings Bank Journal* and *National Savings and Loan League Journal.* Articles of interest to the thrift industry. (BLI, online)

348. *Capitol Banking Review.* Washington, DC: Washington Document Service, 1987—. Weekly.

Newsletter covering Washington legislative and regulatory activities in commercial banking and thrifts.

349. *Credit Union Magazine.* Madison, WI: Credit Union National Association, 1924—. Monthly.

For officers and managers of credit unions. Information on operations, legislation, regulation, marketing and public relations. (PAIS, BLI)

350. *Credit Union News.* New York, 1981—. Bi-weekly.

National newspaper on developments in credit unions.

351. *EFT Report.* Potomac, MD: Phillips, 1978—. Biweekly.

     Newsletter of electronic banking and data communications. Available online.

352. *Euromoney.* London: Euromoney Publications, 1969—. Monthly.

     Articles on the world's capital and money markets. Regular columns of editorial comment, the market place, Tokyo watch, the diary and key figures. (BPI, PAIS, BLI, online)

353. *FDIC Banking Review.* Washington, DC: Federal Deposit Insurance Corporation, 1988—. Quarterly.

     Reviews recent developments in bank supervision and regulation. Special articles dealing with such matters as bank failures and interest rate risks contain considerable statistical information. Supersedes information formerly published in FDIC's *Regulatory Review* and *Banking and Economic Review.*

354. Federal Deposit Insurance Corporation. *Quarterly Banking Profile.* Washington, DC, 1986—. Quarterly.

     Summary report on financial condition of FDIC-insured commercial banks. Shows commercial bank performance for the quarter covered, as well as aggregate condition and income data, and selected indicators.

355. Federal Reserve Bank of Atlanta. *Economic Review.* Atlanta, GA, 1915—. Bi-monthly.

     This, as do the other Federal Reserve banks' reviews, listed below, contains articles of general banking and economic concerns with special emphasis on the regional district. Some of the banks also publish separate statistical bulletins or releases. (BLI, online)

356. Federal Reserve Bank of Boston. *New England Economic Review.* Boston, 1921—. Bi-monthly. (PAIS, BLI, online)

357. Federal Reserve Bank of Chicago. *Economic Perspectives.* Chicago, 1921—. Bi-monthly. (BLI, online)

358. Federal Reserve Bank of Cleveland. *Economic Review.* Cleveland, OH, 1921—. Quarterly. (PAIS, BLI, online)

359. Federal Reserve Bank of Dallas. *Economic Review.* Dallas, TX, 1916—. Bi-monthly. (BLI, online)

360. Federal Reserve Bank of Kansas City. *Economic Review.* Kansas City, MO, 1916—. Monthly. (BPI, PAIS, BLI, online)

361. Federal Reserve Bank of Minneapolis. *Quarterly Review.* Minneapolis, MN, 1977—. Quarterly. (BLI, online)

362. Federal Reserve Bank of New York. *Quarterly Review.* New York, 1915—. Quarterly, formerly monthly. (BPI, PAIS, BLI, online)

363. Federal Reserve Bank of Philadelphia. *Business Review.* Philadelphia, PA, 1918—. Bi-monthly. (PAIS, BLI, online)

364. Federal Reserve Bank of Richmond. *Economic Review*. Richmond, VA, 1914—. Bi-monthly. (BLI, online)

365. Federal Reserve Bank of St. Louis. *Review*. St. Louis, MO, 1917—. Bi-monthly. (BPI, PAIS, BLI, online)

366. Federal Reserve Bank of San Francisco. *Economic Review*. San Francisco, CA, 1921—. Quarterly. (PAIS, BLI, online)

367. *Federal Reserve Bulletin*. Washington, DC: Board of Governors of the Federal Reserve System, 1915—. Monthly.
    Articles discuss current Federal Reserve Board policies and operations, analyze monetary and credit developments and related economic and banking matters. Most of the statistics previously published in the statistical releases are reissued in the "Financial and Business Statistics" section. (BPI, PAIS, BLI, online)

368. *Financial Times*. London, 1888—. Daily with Weekend edition.
    Major international newspaper covering banking and finance worldwide. Each day usually has a special section on the financial situation of a particular country or of a specific aspect of the financial industry. Available online.

369. *Independent Banker*. Sauk Center, MN: Independent Bankers Association, 1950—. Monthly.
    Articles and information for small banks on administration, credit management, marketing, auditing and operation. (PAIS, BLI)

370. *International Financial Statistics.* Washington, DC: International Monetary Fund, 1948—. Monthly with Yearbook.

Principal source of international statistics on all aspects of international and domestic finance. Gives current financial data for most countries. There are tables for 138 countries, as well as for areas and for the world. Includes country charts showing recent changes in important series. The yearbook contains annual data for the past fifteen years or more, plus the previous fifth and tenth year. The yearbook has a separate chart section which shows key time series data on a uniform semi-log scale for twelve years.

371. *Issues in Bank Regulation.* Rolling Meadows, IL: Bank Administration Institute, 1977—. Quarterly.

Information for bankers and bank regulators on regulations and related issues. Features comments by bankers and regulators. (BLI, online)

372. *Journal of Banking and Finance.* Amsterdam, The Netherlands: Elsevier, 1977—. Quarterly.

An international journal of research on financial institutions and the money and capital markets in which they function. Aims at those in academic and other research communities, as well as members of private and public financial institutions who are responsible for operational and policy decisions. (BIS, online)

373. *Journal of Commercial Bank Lending.* Philadelphia, PA: Robert Morris Associates, 1918—. Monthly.

Articles on loan management, credit depart-

ment operation and loan office development.
(BPI, PAIS, BLI, online)

374. *Journal of Financial Services Research.* Norwell,
MA: Kluwer Academic Publishers, 1987—.
Quarterly.
    Articles of theoretical and applied analysis of
financial services institutions, instruments and
markets. Focuses on private and public policy
issues common within the industry in the U.S.
and abroad.

375. *Journal of Money, Credit and Banking.* Columbus,
OH: Ohio State University Press, 1969—. Quar-
terly.
    Scholarly journal on the banking industry.
Includes book reviews. (BPI, PAIS, BLI, online)

376. *Morgan Economic Quarterly.* New York: Morgan
Guaranty Trust, 1984—. Quarterly.
    Articles on the U.S. economy, developments
in financial markets and developments in the
financial services industry.

377. *Savings Institutions.* Chicago: United States
League of Savings Institutions, 1980—.
Monthly.
    Aimed at managers and supervisors of savings
institutions as an aid in the performance of their
jobs. (BPI, BLI)

378. U.S. Office of the Comptroller of the Currency. *Quarterly Journal.* Washington, DC,
1981—. Quarterly.
    Journal of record of the most significant
actions and policies of the Office of the Comptroller of the Currency. Includes policy state-

ments, decisions, selected speeches, interpretations and statistics.

379. U.S. Office of Thrift Supervision. *Journal.* Washington, DC, 1989—. Quarterly.
Continues the monthly journal previously issued by the Federal Home Loan Bank Board. Contains articles of concern to the savings and loan industry, as well as statistics and regulatory information.

380. U.S. Office of Thrift Supervision. *News.* Washington, DC, 1989—. Monthly and Quarterly.
Formerly published by the Federal Home Loan Bank Board. Periodic releases on mortgage rates, earnings of insured thrifts, statistics on operation of Federal Home Loan Banks, and thrift industry activity statistics.

381. *United States Banker.* Cos Cob, CT: Kali Communications, 1891—. Monthly.
Comment and analysis for management in financial services. Includes banking news of the northeastern region. (PAIS, BLI)

382. *The Wall Street Journal.* New York: Dow Jones, 1889—. Daily except Saturday and Sunday.
Leading newspaper on economic and financial matters. Has own index and available online.

383. *The World of Banking.* Washington, DC: World of Banking Publishing Co. Limited, 1982—. Bimonthly.
Originally published by the Bank Administration Institute. Articles deal with concerns of the world banking community. They cover such subjects as operations, internal control, payment

systems, auditing, accounting and security.
(BLI)

D. Services

384. *The Bank Digest.* Washington, DC: Washington Service Bureau. Daily.

Reports on the activities of the regulatory agencies, Department of the Treasury, federal courts, SEC, and Congress.

385. Board of Governors of the Federal Reserve System. *Federal Reserve Regulatory Service.* Washington, DC. 3 vols. Looseleaf. Monthly.

Designed to promote public understanding of the regulatory function of the Federal Reserve System by bringing together the statutes administered by the Board of Governors, as well as the regulations, interpretations, rulings and opinions issued by the Board and its staff.

386. Bureau of National Affairs. *BNA's Banking Report; Legal and Regulatory Developments in the Financial Services Industry.* Washington, DC. Looseleaf. Weekly.

Supersedes its *Washington Financial Reports.* Covers the activities of the regulatory agencies, Congress and the courts. Includes brief notices of new developments in banking regionally, and national and international economic developments. Text material includes agency rulings, court decisions and key legislation as well as special reports. Available online.

387. *Control of Banking.* Englewood Cliffs, NJ: Prentice-Hall. 2 vols. Looseleaf. Bi-weekly.

Report bulletins on new decisions and rulings. Discusses new ideas in banking techniques and methods. Includes the National Bank Law and regulations and rulings of the Comptroller of the Currency. Covers the Federal Reserve Act, deposit insurance and fiscal regulations. Includes the Export Import Bank Act and Bretton Woods. Reports on current matters.

388. *Depository Institutions Performance Directory.* Boston: Warren, Gorham & Lamont. 3 vols. Quarterly updates and year-end annual.

Covers more than 20,000 banks, thrifts, and bank holding companies. Data include information on assets, earnings, loans and deposits with rankings.

389. *DIALOG.* Palo Alto, CA: DIALOG Information Services, Inc.

Online service accessing many databases including *ABI/INFORM, American Banker, Economic Literature Index, Financial Times, FINIS,* and the publications by Moody's and Standard & Poor's services.

390. *Dow Jones News/Retrieval.* Princeton, NJ: Dow Jones & Company, Inc. Updated frequently during the day.

Full-text online coverage of articles from *The Wall Street Journal* and *Barron's,* and many regional and trade publications, online information from Standard & Poor's, Merrill Lynch, Bureau of National Affairs and up-to-date news on stock and other market activities.

391. *FDIC Enforcement Decisions.* Englewood Cliffs, NJ: Prentice-Hall. 2 vols. Looseleaf.

Designed to help comply with FDIC requirements. Publishes decisions and reports on what
FDIC looks for in carrying out its bank oversight
functions, and how past problems were han-
dled.

392. *Federal Banking Law Reports.* Chicago: Commerce Clearing House. 6 vols. Looseleaf.
Weekly.
Covers federal bank and savings and loan
controls. Reports on statutes, legislative developments and new provisions. Publishes regulations, circulars and bulletins issued by administrative agencies.

393. Mead Data Central. *LEXIS/NEXIS.* Dayton, OH.
Two major online databases. LEXIS is mainly
a legal service, but contains full text of a number
of publications related to banking. NEXIS
contains full text of many newspapers, including
The New York Times, periodicals, wire services,
newsletters and government information and
regulation.

394. *NewsNet.* Bryn Mawr, PA: NewsNet Inc.
Online bibliographic data for more than 360
newsletters and other news and information
services. Includes *American Banker, Banking Regulator, Credit Union Regulator, EFT Report, Financial Services Report* and *State Capitals: Banking
Policies.*

395. Norton, Joseph Jude, and Whitley, Sherry
Castle, eds. *Banking Law Manual.* New York:
Matthew Bender. 1 vol. Looseleaf. Annual.
Basic legal reference for bank managers,
students or others concerned with banking

institutions. Analyzes the regulatory framework within which banking institutions operate. Illustrates their powers and legal responsibilities in all aspects of their operations. Includes bibliographies.

396. Schlichtung, William H.; Rice, Terry; and Cooper, Jeffrey. *Banking Law*. New York: Matthew Bender. 10 vols. Looseleaf. Annual.

Each volume edited by various experts, and together provides a comprehensive coverage of laws, regulations and cases concerned with national banking. Index volume contains tables of statutes and tables of cases.

APPENDIX A:

ACRONYMS AND ABBREVIATIONS

ABA	American Bankers Association
ACH	Automated Clearing House
ADP	Automatic Data Processing
AIB	American Institute of Banking
AICPA	American Institute of Certified Public Accountants
ARCB	Association of Reserve City Bankers
ATM	Automated Teller Machines
BAI	Bank Administration Institute
BHC	Bank Holding Company
BIF	Bank Insurance Fund
BIS	Bank for International Settlements
BLI	Bank Literature Index
BPI	Business Periodicals Index
CEO	Chief Executive Officer
CFO	Chief Financial Officer
CFR	Code of Federal Regulations
CMC	Commission on Money and Credit
CPA	Certified Public Accountant
CU	Credit Union
CUNA	Credit Union National Association
DIA	Depository Institutions Act of 1982 (Garn-St. Germain)
DIDMCA	Depository Institutions Deregulation and Monetary Control Act of 1980
EDP	Electronic Data Processing

EFT	Electronic Funds Transfer
FASB	Financial Accounting Standards Board
FDIC	Federal Deposit Insurance Corporation
Fed	Federal Reserve Bank or System
FFIEC	Federal Financial Institutions Examination Council
FHFB	Federal Housing Finance Board
FHLBB	Federal Home Loan Bank Board
FHLMC	Federal Home Loan Mortgage Corporation
FINE	Financial Institutions and the Nation's Economy (Study)
FOMC	Federal Open Market Committee
FSLIC	Federal Savings and Loan Insurance Corporation
IBA	Institute of Bank Administration
IRS	Internal Revenue Service
LDCs	Less Developed Countries
NCUA	National Credit Union Administration
NOW	Negotiable Order of Withdrawal
NTIS	National Technical Information Service
OECD	Organization for Economic Cooperation and Development
OTS	Office of Thrift Supervision
PAIS	Public Affairs Information Service
POS	Point-of-Sale
RefCorp	Resolution Funding Corporation
RTC	Resolution Trust Corporation
S&L	Savings and Loan
SAIF	Savings Association Insurance Fund
SEC	Securities and Exchange Commission
SMSA	Standard Metropolitan Statistical Area
UCC	Uniform Commercial Code

APPENDIX B:

BANKING LANDMARKS: A CHRONOLOGY

1781	Bank of North America established by Robert Morris.
1791-1811	First Bank of the United States chartered by Congress.
1816-1836	Second Bank of the United States chartered by Congress.
1863-1864	National Bank Act. Established procedure for chartering banks by federal government.
1876	U.S. Monetary Commission. Report and Documents published 1877-1879.
1912	National Monetary Commission. Report published known as the Aldrich Plan.
1913	Federal Reserve Act. Federal Reserve System established.
1927	McFadden Act. Prohibited interstate banking.
1932	Federal Home Loan Bank Act. Established central credit facility for thrift institutions.
1932	Glass-Steagall Act. Separated commercial and investment banking.
1933	Banking Act. Established Federal Deposit Insurance Corporation.

1934   Federal Savings and Loan Insurance Corporation Act. Created facility to insure federally and state-chartered thrift institutions.

1935   Banking Act. Made certain changes in the structure of the Federal Reserve System.

1949   Commission on Organization of the Executive Branch of the Government. Known as the Hoover Commission. Studied the organization and function of governmental departments and agencies.

1950   Federal Deposit Insurance Act. FDIC originally established by Banking Act of 1933. This separate law provides for insurance for deposits held by state and national banks and members of the Federal Reserve System.

1956   Bank Holding Company Act. Named Federal Reserve regulator of companies owning two or more banks.

1960   Bank Merger Act. Disallowed merger of FDIC insured banks with noninsured banks without FDIC approval.

1961   Commission on Money and Credit. Report based on studies of the financial structure of the U.S.

1962   Advisory Committee on Banking. Report, known as the Saxon Report, recommended changes in the national banking system.

1966   Financial Institutions Supervisory Act. Strengthened powers of bank supervisors.

1968   Truth in Lending Act. Regulated interest rate advertising.

1970   Bank Holding Company Act Amendment.

	Extended Federal Reserve regulatory powers to one-bank holding companies.
1970	Federal Credit Union Act. Provided for chartering and supervising federal credit unions by NCUA.
1971	President's Commission on Financial Structure and Regulation. Known as the Hunt Commission, recommended changes in the regulation of financial institutions.
1975	Financial Institutions and the Nation's Economy. The FINE study recommended a number of changes in the structure and regulation of financial institutions.
1977	National Commission on Electronic Funds Transfers. Report concerned the orderly development of private and public EFT systems.
1978	Financial Institutions Regulatory and Interest Rate Control Act. Increased regulation of insider trading.
1978	Full Employment and Balanced Growth Act. Required Federal Reserve to report semi-annually to Congress on monetary policy objectives.
1978	International Banking Act. Put foreign and domestic banks on equal footing.
1980	Depository Institutions and Monetary Control Act. Required Federal Reserve to price its financial services available to all depository institutions; and established reserve requirements to all eligible financial institutions.
1980	Interagency Task Force on Thrift Institutions. Report analyzed problems faced by thrift institutions.

1982   Depository Institutions Act. Known as the
            Garn-St Germain Act, deregulated some
            activities of banks and nonbank banks.

1984   Task Group on Regulation of Financial
            Services. Known as the Bush Commit-
            tee. Report concerned the federal finan-
            cial regulatory system.

1987   Competitive Equality in Banking Act and
            Expedited Funds Availability Act. Rede-
            fined nonbank banks and expanded
            some bank powers.

1989   Financial Institutions Reform, Recovery
            and Enforcement Act. Familiarly called
            the Thrift Bailout.

APPENDIX C:

REGULATORY AGENCIES AND OFFICES

1. Agencies

Board of Governors of the Federal Reserve System
Twentieth Street and Constitution Avenue N.W.
Washington, DC 20551

Principal function to supervise domestic and international operations of all member banks.

Comptroller of the Currency
490 L'Enfant Plaza East S.W.
Washington, DC 20219

Administrator of national banks, promulgates rules and regulations and exercises general supervision and examination of national banks.

Federal Deposit Insurance Corporation
550 Seventeenth Street N.W.
Washington, DC 20429

Insures deposits of national banks and state Federal Reserve member banks, supervises and examines state nonmember banks.

National Credit Union Administration
1776 G Street N.W.
Washington, DC 20456

Charters, supervises and examines federal credit unions.

Securities and Exchange Commission
450 Fifth Steet N.W.
Washington, DC 20549

Regulates securities markets.

Treasury Department
1500 Pennsylvania Avenue N.W.
Washington, DC 20220

Office of Thrift Supervision now under its jurisdiction.

2. Offices

Bank Insurance Fund
550 Seventeenth Street N.W.
Washington, DC 20429

New name for Federal Deposit Insurance Corporation's fund that insures bank deposits up to $100,000.

Federal Housing Finance Board
1700 G Sreet N.W.
Washington, DC 20552

Oversees the Home Loan Bank System.

Federal Savings and Loan Insurance Corporation Resolution Fund
550 Seventeenth Street N.W.
Washington, DC 20429

Manages remaining assets and liabilities of 200 savings and loan banks taken over by FSLIC prior to 1989.

Office of Thrift Supervision
1700 G Street N.W.
Washington, DC 20552

Formerly Federal Home Loan Bank Board. Institutes new regulations, charters federal S&Ls, supervises state-chartered banks and S&L holding companies.

Resolution Trust Corporation
550 Seventeenth Street N.W.
Washington, DC 20429

Managed by the FDIC. Mandate is to close and sell more than 400 sick S&Ls.

Savings Association Insurance Fund
550 Seventeenth Street N.W.
Washington, DC 20429

Formerly Federal Savings and Loan Insurance Corporation. Insures deposits up to $100,000 at thrift institutions, will manage assets and liabilities of insolvent S&Ls after 1992.

APPENDIX D:

SELECTED LIST OF
TRADE ASSOCIATIONS

American Bankers Association
1129 Connecticut Avenue N.W.
Washington, DC 20036

Association of Bank Holding Companies
730 Fifteenth Street N.W.
Washington, DC 20005

Association of Reserve City Bankers
1710 Rhode Island Avenue N.W., Suite 500
Washington, DC 20036

Bank Administration Institute
60 Gould Center
Rolling Meadows, IL 60008

Bank Marketing Association
309 W. Washington Street
Chicago, IL 60606

Consumer Bankers Association
1300 N. Seventeenth Street
Arlington, VA 22209

Credit Union Executives Society
2801 Coho Street, Suite 300
Madison, WI 53714

Credit Union National Association
P.O. Box 431
Madison, WI 53701

Independent Bankers Association of America
One Thomas Circle N.W., Suite 950
Washington, DC 20005

Institute of International Bankers
280 Park Avenue
New York, NY 10017

Institute of International Finance
2000 Pennsylvania Avenue, Suite 2267
Washington, DC 20006

National Association of Bank Women
500 N. Michigan Avenue, Suite 1400
Chicago, IL 60601

National Bankers Association
122 C Street N.W., Suite 240
Washington, DC 20001

National Council of Savings Institutions
1101 Fifteenth Street N.W.
Washington, DC 20005

Robert Morris Associates
1 Liberty Place
Philadelphia, PA 19103

Securities Industry Association
120 Broadway
New York, NY 10271

United States League of Savings Institutions
1709 New York Avenue N.W.
Washington, DC 20006

AUTHOR INDEX

TITLE INDEX